LEMON JAIL

LEMON JAIL

ON THE ROAD WITH THE REPLACEMENTS

BILL SULLIVAN

UNIVERSITY OF MINNESOTA PRESS

MINNEAPOLIS LONDON

Photographs on pages 22, 31, and 32 by Wayne Valdez. All other photographs appear courtesy of the author.

Published by the University of Minnesota Press
111 Third Avenue South, Suite 290
Minneapolis, MN 55401-2520
http://www.upress.umn.edu

Printed in the United States of America on acid-free paper

The University of Minnesota is an equal-opportunity educator and employer.

27 26 25 24 23 22 21   10 9 8 7 6 5 4 3 2 1

Library of Congress Cataloging-in-Publication Data
Sullivan, Bill, author.
Lemon jail : on the road with the Replacements / Bill Sullivan.
Minneapolis : University of Minnesota Press, [2018]
Identifiers: LCCN 2017051774 (print) | ISBN 978-1-5179-0169-1 (hc) | ISBN 978-1-5179-1276-5 (pb)
Subjects: LCSH: Sullivan, Bill, 1960– | Stagehands—United States—Biography. | Replacements (Musical group).
Classification: LCC ML429.S95 A3 2018 (print) | DDC 782.42166092 [B]—dc23
LC record available at https://lccn.loc.gov/2017051774

For the Gone But Not Forgottens

CONTENTS

The ribs of the vehicle were exposed like a pre–World War II bomber and they rattled in the wind as we hauled ass down the highway. Inside there were seven of us just like the samurai huddled against the cold, sharing what blankets and sleeping bags we had. Our feet were freezing in our less-than-sensible footwear. No hats or scarves because they weren't cool.

Carton had acquired our van from a high school friend's older brother who was well known in our old neighborhood for being able to find what you needed. Unlike most of the touring groups of the time, we didn't build any fancy lofts or structures in the van we called Bert. The seats had long since been removed, and we simply laid the amps, cases, and cabinets on the floor of the van with patio chair cushions as padding. We huddled on upside-down speaker cabinets and leaned against drum hardware boxes. The boom box that we used, sans an installed music system, was at full blast in order to compete with the howl of the road cutting through the uncarpeted floor.

In any van with sliding doors there's a step with a groove in it that the door runner slides along. We called this the trough, and it became the resting place for all of the garbage accumulated as we drove down the road. Beer cans, cig butts, half-eaten sandwiches, and chicken bones mingled with wrappers and urine. First, Paul would get on his knees and try to pee out a small hole between the trough and the door, but soon he and Tommy just peed in the trough. When we got down south, it was so hot we would prop the door open with a board and Paul would stand in the opening while someone would hold on to his belt and he'd pee onto the highway and mostly along the side of the van where Chris had drawn Fred Flintstone in Sharpie, flexing his bicep and smirking, saying, "C'mon, Pussy." Anytime you stop at a truck stop on tour you lose an average of thirty minutes, and even a rest area would cause a considerable delay in the trip between gigs. Just pulling over to the side of the road was out of the question—*the cops would have had a field day with us pissing on the highway. So we pissed in the trough. It required flexibility and Paul had the best talent for it. One knee on the floor, one leg out to the side, and aim for the little hole in the back that drained out to the highway. Bob was the worst at it and did it only when absolutely necessary. The resulting landfill in Bert became the band's calling card. When we arrived at a venue, the band would open the door before I put Bert into park and, kicking the trash out on the sidewalk, announce to anyone in earshot, "We're here!"*

This was Bert: a late '70s Ford Econoline. This is where I spent the most important days of my life. In this crappy stinking lemon jail.

GET OUT OF THE BASEMENT

We're at the sold-out Orlando Arena, opening for Tom Petty and the Heartbreakers. It's 1989, and the Replacements are on the doorstep of fame, possibly their only chance to kick down the door of rock-and-roll radio and take their rightful place in the mainstream. The band had finally "made it." But here was Paul flapping his arms like a chicken. *Baaaaak,* he called off mic. *Baaaaak.* Scratching at the dirt, flapping his imaginary chicken wings, cajoling the roadie to come onstage and take over lead vocals. It's not that the show was going poorly: it was just no fun, a big cavernous room with twenty thousand classic rockers staring indifferently at the stage. And now, as Paul often did when the show was going south or his voice was sore or he just didn't give a shit—or, as in tonight's case, if it was just a big laugh at "rock and roll"—he had decided to prove that even with his roadie on vocals he could fool the masses to their feet. That roadie was me.

Six years earlier, in April 1983, I had quit my job as night guard at the Walker Art Center in Minneapolis and cashed my final paycheck before climbing into a converted phone company van with Paul Westerberg, Bob Stinson, Tommy Stinson, and Chris Mars, along with their Faithful Roadie Tom "Carton" Carlson and Intrepid Manager Peter Jesperson, on the Replacements' first national tour. I had been helping out the band as an unpaid loader and driver for a while as they roamed from Duluth to Madison, but this time they were headed east to New York City. I had lied to Paul, telling him I was a good guy to have around and was willing to work for

nothing. Somehow he was convinced and in turn convinced the manager to bring me along.

I tried to make myself useful. Hauling amps and shit, finding parties and a place to crash (often the same place). As it turned out, I was a pretty good roadie. I seemed to be able to walk—or better yet, straddle—the line between legal and stupid.

On some nights I sang lead vocals. I didn't sing Replacements songs. Instead, I sang replacement Replacements songs. It would start with a blown fuse or speaker, maybe an intermittent cable, and I'd be up there fuckin with it, not because I knew what I was doing so much as there was no one else to do it, so I figured if you switch out and wiggle shit and move it around, things just might start working again. While I was up there, often in an uncomfortable silence, I would start to tell a joke or two and the next thing I knew Paul or Chris would grab the guitar and start me up on one of my numbers. Usually it was songs from movie soundtracks like "Do the Clam" or "If I Only Had a Brain."

Before we left on this first national tour, the new management had insisted it would be better if I stayed off the stage. But unfortunately for them, whatever you asked for with the Replacements, you usually got the opposite. One such example was the time the label called me and told me that reports from the road detailed that I was the one who was starting all the trouble, doing all the damage and drinking all the whiskey, and that, because of these reports, I was fired. I thought it was weird that Paul hadn't done it himself; after all, he had fired and rehired me and everyone else many times already. After a couple weeks, Paul called and asked where I had been the last couple shows. I told him I had been fired. He told me I was most certainly not, that only he could fire someone from the 'Mats, and he wanted me to go up to Fargo with them that weekend. No shock to me he chose that show, as the gig was at a redneck hunting bar, opening for a popular cover band whose lead singer had just gotten the call-up from the band Head East. Clearly, they felt they needed backup on this one,

and while there was no actual fighting that night, things were pretty hairy. After the show, preaching in tongues with the door and windows wide open, garbage and cig ash swirling around me, I was christened "Father O'Ruckus." Once Paul gave you a nickname, you were here to stay.

And here we were six years later, and this was not just another club tour. We were opening for the Heartbreakers in arenas across the country and there were expectations now. The label and the promoter all had protocols, and some things were just not gonna be tolerated. And now Paul's strumming the opening chords of my go-to-song of go-to-songs: Alice Cooper's "Eighteen." There he was in front of twenty thousand perplexed rednecks repeating the opening bars over and over, calling me out, taunting me with the universally irresistible chicken taunt.

Before the tour I had promised the band's new major label and big-time managers that I would stay off the stage, that we would behave like a professional outfit. The Petty tour was seen as the band's big break, but I had been there for all of the band's "big breaks"—the cover of *Village Voice*, a major record deal—only to see the band remain in the same mid-level cut-out bin reserved for bands that no one understood, bands that the industry veterans despised and envied at the same time. And tonight in Tom Petty's home state, on the first night of the tour, it seemed the whole industry was watching. Clearly, the new management and major label reps were, the very people I had promised I would stay off the stage and do my best to behave.

But here was Paul raising his middle finger to them all, on the big stage. But here in the house the Mouse built the band was flat, the crowd was flat, the set was flat. So I did what I had always done when things weren't going well. I tried to make it fun. Running onstage, I grabbed the microphone and ripped into the opening verse. They erupted, leather-clad arms thrust in the air, twenty thousand lighters burning in the dark and half a dozen girls in the front row lifting their shirts for my approval. I was an instant hit.

At load-out, two women in wheelchairs approached and asked if we could arrange for them to meet Tom. We explained that we were the opening band and had no pull. At that moment Petty emerged from the stage door and strode across the parking lot toward his bus, causing one of the girls to jump up out of her chair and sprint past security toward him, at the same time pushing the other girl's chair out of the lock position and down the hill face first into the bumper of our truck. I reached out to help her and she tossed me aside and furiously pushed her chair toward her friend who was struggling with security, kicking and swearing like a banshee.

Later, as we sat in a nearby bar, people were buying me drinks and slapping me on the back, telling me I was great. Someone asked me if I was scared up there.

"Terrified," I replied.

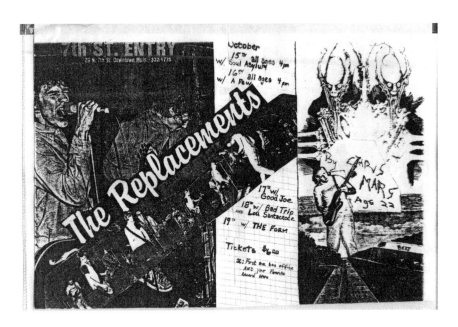

"Guess you won't wanna do that again."

"Are you kidding?" I replied. "I wanna do that every night for the rest of my fucking life."

As it turned out, *Rolling Stone* was writing a tour diary of the Petty tour, and I would be featured in the first paragraph. What happened later that night, in the early morning darkness, didn't make it into the article, however, as no one was around to witness our truck as it swerved off the highway in the dark. Shaken awake when we veered into the median, I looked to my left and saw Brendan McCabe, my partner in crime on the last couple tours, asleep at the wheel. I could smell fresh cut grass, the dew sprinkling the windshield as we sped down the median. Slowly, the reality of the situation became clear to me. We were off the road, our forty-foot Ryder truck cutting through the sawgrass that separates Interstate 70 on the Florida/Georgia line.

With my right hand I took firm hold of the wheel while softly placing my other hand on Brendan's shoulder and said, "Wake up, man." He opened his eyes and for just a moment looked confused, then removed my hand from the steering wheel and eased us back onto the highway. As we speed under an overpass he spoke. "In my dream," he said, "I was back in Queens, mowing the lawn."

Back to the Beginning

I guess it all started, before the Replacements, before the Lemon Jail, when I saw the Ramones in Madison in 1979. I jumped into a car with a group of people I had never met, with twenty bucks and an envelope of magic mushrooms in my pocket. Headliners' Night Club, the special of the night, was forty ounces of beer for fifty cents—buying two, I wandered up to the stage just as the lead singer of the local hair metal band opening the show leaned forward over the audience, shook his mane, and let out his best high-pitch wail, getting a face full of beer and rain of spit from the punks in the crowd for his efforts. When the Ramones came onstage, it was 1–2–3–4 and I was caught up in my first slam dance, taking body shots and elbows to the face. After the show I found my way to the car. With my shirt torn and my pants covered in beer and mud, my car mates were not impressed, and driving back in an uncomfortable silence I held a paper bag near my mouth the whole way. I shared a small house off campus and had forgotten my key, so I had to climb in the window. I drunkenly rolled over the sill and landed facedown in a puddle of bong water and puked. I remember thinking, for the first but not last time, *This is what I want to do every night for the rest of my life.*

When I woke up the next morning, I packed a bag with my favorite shirts and hitchhiked back to Minneapolis, where I ran into a junior high classmate named Tom Carlson, with whom I'd been part of a loose-knit group of outsiders in school who smoked weed and cruised the lakes listening to rock. Tom got me a job working at the Walker Art Center as a night guard. He had been hanging with the art punks for a couple years at that point, and Tom introduced me to the scene while I began to help hump gear for local bands and crew chiefs. As night guard at the Walker, I was able to spend all night listening to Tom's mix tapes of Punk Rock 101, all the while going through the magazines left out in the office of the Walker's brilliant music curator, Tim Carr. Learning about "The Kitchen" scene in New York City, I listened to tapes of shows from Patti Smith and Television as well as the Suburbs and the Suicide Commandos. It was a treasure trove in his unkempt office, and under every book was another discovery.

I was in the guard room at the Walker listening to the Replacements do an interview on KDWB, and the interviewer asked Bob what gave him his inspiration to be a musician, and he responded: a shovel, a book of matches, and the hedges around my house. Years later I would ask his brother Tommy about it, and he told me that when they were kids Bob used to pretend the shovel was his guitar and the hedges were his amp, and that one day he lit his "amps" on fire and nearly burned the house down.

In between guard shifts I would go home and watch Letterman's morning show before going to bed around 10 a.m. Getting up that evening at 6 or 7 p.m., I would have some food and hit the town, trying to see every show that was happening. I ran from club to club to bar to house party, and when I had to work, I kept a uniform and shoes stashed at work to change into just out of sight of the security cameras. All night on shift I would listen to punk and stare at Hopper, usually on mushrooms.

On the night my worlds collided, the Replacements played at the Walker in its stark plain performance hall opening for Curtiss A, and I put it all together. "Carton," as Tom was now called, had gotten his name because he had been carting the Replacements' gear around for them. The band's manager, Peter Jesperson, would hold court late nights at his apartment in the Modesto building after the CC Club closed, where he was known for spinning records and dropping knowledge to the few who were lucky enough to be invited. I slipped in one night and was sitting quietly in the corner when he dropped a needle on Artful Dodger, and when the song tailed out, I mumbled that I had seen them. And that cracked the ice.

At first, I just tagged along, carrying drums and amps into shows to avoid the cover. But as time went on I became a fixture around the band. I was mostly acting like a jackass, slamming with the punks and putting Paul's mic stand back up when it got knocked over. Standing at the backstage entrance at one of my first shows with the Replacements, I was approached by someone who told me he was Paul's high school friend. I told him to hold on and relayed the message to Paul in the dressing room, to which his response was that he had no friends in high school.

One night they all showed up at my apartment, and I found myself helping pull off the coolest guerrilla advertising campaign, stamping THE REPLACEMENTS STINK on a couple thousand blank sleeves. It was 1983, and I was living with Carton in

Sorry ma,
Went to see
The
Replacements
Billy

music?
8pm.

THE
REPLACEMENTS

Feb. 13, 1983

THE
WHOLE coffeehouse

basement of coffman
union

north Minneapolis, and one day everything we had was stolen except Carton's massive record collection. As the only registered resident Carton got a nice check. As an unregistered boondocker I got nothing.

At that time, Carton had been writing STINK on every Replacements poster we walked by. Since our apartment was empty, Peter and the band brought blank sleeves and rubber stamps over to our place, and we sat and stamped covers until our hands blistered. At one point the stamp handles broke off and we used our palms until they blistered as well. As we got drunker, Paul began putting cig butts and other trash inside random sleeves, which ballooned into him marking up the covers and even watercoloring one cover. I was told the band would be doing a tour on the East Coast after the release of the latest EP, and I knew then that I had to get on that tour. Every time I saw Paul after that, I lied and lobbied for the gig. *I'll work for nothing,* I told him. *I'll stay sober and drive,* I told him. *I'll watch your back,* I told him. *Really, who do you want in a bar fight?*

Out of the Basement

Pulling into the Stinsons' driveway at the house made famous on the cover of *Let It Be*—the same house where Peter Jesperson had sat in the bushes and listened to the band practice when he first heard their demo tape, and where I also sat in that same window well before I went in and just listened, sometimes hearing my old favorites and sometimes hearing a song for the first time, as was the case with "You're My Favorite Thing"—pulling into that driveway before that first tour, the band had already hauled the obvious stuff out to the curb: amps, cabinets, drums. I let myself into the Stinsons' kitchen.

Passing through, I would always give Anita Stinson the Eddie Haskell routine, but I truly liked and respected Mrs. Stinson. I never really saw any other part of their house besides the basement and the kitchen, but I always felt like I knew its layout from Bob and Tommy's harrowing stories of their childhood, which were not too different from mine in general, but while they did start from what I thought of as normal, they strayed far. What I got out of it mostly was that Bob really cared for and protected his little brother, and even if he was heavy-handed in his tutorship of Tommy, the result speaks for itself, as Tommy would become one of America's great rock musicians and an iconic star in his own right.

Into the basement—one that the band would soon discard for a real practice space, something every band dreams of—I ducked in around the octopus furnace that was stuck in the middle of the room, its asbestos tentacles reaching out toward Paul's vocal mic, Bob's pedals, and Tommy's jumps. Only Chris seemed in an area that couldn't be described as a biohazard, if only because he was three feet lower due to sitting at the kit.

That day I did the first idiot check—that's what we called the last run-through to make sure you were not being an idiot and leaving something behind—packing everything I found so that if Paul asked for it later, I had it at hand, no matter how minor. A capo, a cord, a snare piece, or string, I packed it, basically cleaning out Anita's basement for the first time in years. I even took out the trash.

The day we were leaving, my mom packed our family's old red Coleman cooler that for years we'd taken on family picnics, filled with ham and turkey and a block of American cheese and some milk cartons she cleaned out and refilled with water, freezing them into ice blocks to keep the food fresh. She also included bread and condiments and a ziplock bag that contained a couple dozen of her chocolate chip cookies that had been famously good for barter in the lunchrooms of southwest Minneapolis for almost anything you wanted. She did all this even though she didn't understand my fascination with the band she liked to call the Placemats. She could only be encouraging.

It was not unlike years later, when Conor Oberst's mother would ask me, "What do you do? Try and stop him, and risk never seeing him again?

Or you could encourage him and maybe see him again." My mom gave me bags of clean jockeys and socks along with a one-way airline ticket voucher, "in case you don't like it." My father? He wrote me a "group accidental death" policy at his insurance company.

Just east of Minneapolis down Interstate I-94 you hit Black River Falls, where a Giant Orange Moose greets you with promises of Gifts and Cheese. While Carton filled the tank and Peter found a pay phone, the band and I wandered through a walk-in cooler stocked with an impressive array of beer. The band nervously fingered the fresh $20 bill that their manager had handed them. *Per diem*, the lifeblood of a touring band. Other than the occasional dinner buy-out, it was the only thing that got you by. Morning coffee, $1.50. Pack-a-day habit, $2.50. Fast food, $5.00, a couple beers and a whiskey, $7.50. Chips, breath mints, and other incidentals, and it was gone.

I had just cashed my last paycheck from the security job and after purchasing some weed on the way out of town I had just about $200 left. That

Get Out of the Basement

put me on a tight budget for two weeks out east. But figuring my mom's sandwiches as a buffer, I grabbed a couple of six packs of my favorite Wisconsin beer, Point, the cool blue cans bright and shiny with their promise of brewing excellence, and returned to the van, putting them in the red Coleman. That oughta last me, I remember thinking at the time. Tommy was too young, Chris only drank on occasion and then to excess, Peter liked Scotch, and Carton was driving. I figured Paul would want a couple. I didn't count on Bob.

By the time we were bypassing Chicago, Paul and I were drunk, crooning along to the radio. Bob seemed to be able to eat and drink as fast as we just drank but never seemed any different from usual. The empties landed back in the cooler, as did the cigarette butts and other scraps, turning my mother's generosity into an unappetizing Superfund cleanup. Paul handled the radio dial. When it was corporate rock he would decide what was listenable. Bonnie Tyler NO, Stray Cats YES, David Bowie YES. Eddy Grant? Uh, OKAY.

The Eastern Whirl of '83

In rural areas the oldies stations ruled. Having worked summers at the lakes in Minneapolis as a kid, I knew every song by heart, and when Hurricane Smith's "Oh Babe, What Would You Say?" came on, I plugged my nose and sang along in an old-timey voice.

That first night in Detroit, the band opened for the Neats from Boston at Detroit's City Club, a goth dive and dance club in the basement of the Leyland Hotel once thought to be the final resting place of Jimmy Hoffa. It was still thought to be haunted, so Chris and I took it upon ourselves to explore. The upper floors were closed off by plywood, but that was easily pried away to access the kippled walls of the old ballroom and the not-entirely-empty pool. No ghosts, no Hoffa. The men's room in the club was a shit hole, so since the doors weren't open yet, I checked out the ladies' room. The toilets had seats—that was a plus—but there was no paper

THE REPLACEMENTS

1983 EASTERN WHIRL

——— mpls ———
UPPER DECK
saturday 4/2

——— detroit ———
CITY CLUB *NEATS*
saturday 4/9

——— new york ———
FOLK CITY
wednesday 4/13

——— albany n.y. ———
CHATEAU
thurs. 4/14

——— philadelphia ———
EAST SIDE CLUB
fri. 4/15

——— nyc ———
DANCETERIA
saturday 4/16

GUILDERSLEEVES *HÜSKER DÜ*
sunday **4/17**

——— brooklyn ———
ZAPPA'S *FLIPPER*
wednesday 4/20

——— bridgeport ct. ———
TOGA'S
thursday 4/21

——— hoboken n.j. ———
MAXWELLS
friday 4/22

——— boston ———
THE RAT
saturday 4/23/83

anywhere to be found, not even a bev-nap on the bar, and I was desperately seeking Charmin at this point. I told the band I was going on a cig run to pick up Paul a pack of True Blues.

Nearly every building was boarded up or burned down in the neighborhood, like they never cleaned up after the riots. After passing on a few dive bars with passed-out patrons and surly staff, I came across a small bodega, and the clerk sold me a roll of Scott tissue, spinning my roll and change around on a bulletproof lazy Susan. I race-walked back and slipped into the ladies' room, hoping for a miracle and some solitude, but was soon joined in the next stall by a young woman, at least judging by her shoes. At that point stage fright had won out, but, ever the gentleman, I shared my roll under the wall before she could see my face. After the show the manager introduced me to a friend, who looking down at my boots, told him that we had already met.

Opening the show that night was a local band called Hurricane Irv. I thought Paul should acknowledge them from the stage since they had brought in much of the crowd. He obliged by saying he wanted to thank Hurricane Smith. The crowd howled back at him "Irv...Irv!" He corrected himself by saying thanks to Irv Smith for opening the show.

Meeting the Neats was the highlight of the night. They were part of the Boston music scene that I had been following closely since I had started a pen-pal relationship with the Del Fuegos by sending them a note to the address printed on the back of their single "I Can't Sleep." According to Lilli, my note read: "Our bands should be friends."

After the show, Peter checked us into a couple of rooms at the nearby Book–Cadillac Hotel, which had housed Jimmy Hoffa's union offices, and we were told that his ghost was still haunting the rooms. Chris was carrying a guitar on the escalator, and it got stuck on the landing, pinning his leg between the case and the moving stairway. The automatic shutdown activated, causing flashing lights and alarms, and security arrived accusing us of breaking the escalator. Of course.

Me and Lilli in Boston

We were supposed to drive to Hoboken the next morning, but R.E.M. was opening later that same night in Detroit for the English Beat at the Grand Circus Theater. Peter convinced everyone (meaning Paul) that it would be fun to go to the show. It wouldn't be long before I would figure out that *any* sidetrack on tour with the Replacements was a bad idea.

For Peter this was a particularly poor decision. Sitting in a littered parking lot waiting for his return with our passes, Paul muttered more than once that we should just leave him. When Peter did return, and we were escorted into the theater, it was just in time to see the stage crew lower the proscenium onto the theater's iconic Wurlitzer pipe organ, crushing it with a dolefully sustained note. At one point in history, it was the largest pipe organ in the country—now it was a little smaller. As the union crew ran around shouting and cursing, we were herded out of the room, and, just like with the escalator, I sensed that we were somehow being blamed.

Get Out of the Basement

On to New York

In order for Tommy, who was sixteen years old, to come on tour, he had to get out of school and the manager be given some sort of guardianship over the lad. When we arrived in Hoboken to begin our siege on New York, I began to have an inkling as to why there had been no resistance to my coming along.

Peter had arranged lodging for himself and his ward as well as Paul. Carton had made plans to take the van into the city and stay with his girlfriend's sister, who had a blossoming career in performance and dance but, more important to this story, access to parking. My brother Dave had an apartment on Washington Street in Hoboken underneath the Carmel and Three Guys from Italy. Chris, Bob, and I stayed there. The cockroaches were huge: when you turned on the kitchen lights the whole counter looked like it was moving as they scurried into the cut. Bob staked a claim to the couch and TV and only got up long enough to relieve himself or go out for a tall boy and a Blimpie. I wandered around Hoboken checking out the cheap bars. Everywhere we went Mars would draw TV characters on the walls of the dressing rooms, usually Fred Flintstone and sometimes Jed Clampett. One night he was working on an intricate sketch of Siamese twin aliens, and when he made one alien's inner organs different from the other alien's organs, he crumpled up the paper and threw it in the trashcan. I retrieved it and had him sign the bottom.

It turns out getting into a parking lot in Manhattan is only part of the equation—getting your vehicle out is the other. Not knowing this, Carton was late for load-in for our most important show of the tour—in fact, the show the whole tour revolved around, the Music for Dozens showcase at the famed Folk City in the West Village. The series had introduced indie acts like Sonic Youth and Dumptruck to the dozens who attended each show. Presented semiweekly, the bills were a departure from Folk City's usual fare of singer-songwriters and classic folk and were assembled by

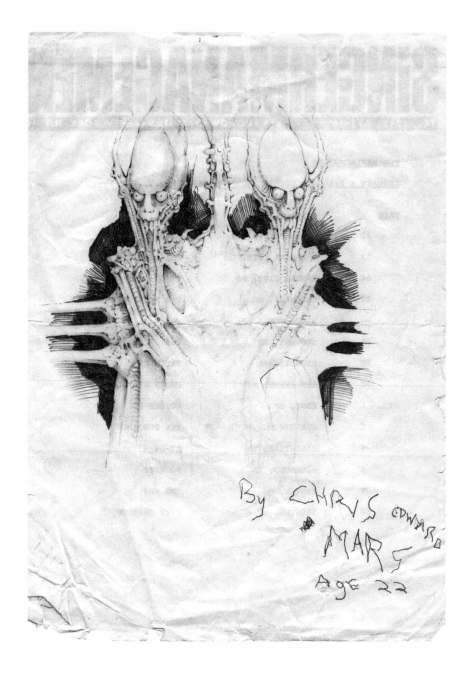

By CHRIS EDWARD
MARS
Age 22

a group of New York rock writers including Ira Kaplan. The flyer for our show was designed by no less than famed artist and musician Georgia Hubley, and the audience would include the East Coast's finest and most influential music critics. So what? The Del Fuegos were on the bill along with the Del-Lords, who were a very professional punk band with the right outfits and the general polished look of the Lower East Side. The Fuegos, who I loved, were ratty like us, perhaps a little staged (they were from New Hampshire), with a solid rhythm section of Tom Lloyd and a drummer, Steve Morrell, who could have been from Duluth or the West Bank of Minneapolis.

As I remember it, we went on loud and late, and the venue staff turned the soundboard off and the house lights on like they were on the same switch. And I was told we would most likely never play Folk City again.

We would in fact be allowed another show at Folk City on our return trip the following year. We had played a rec room in Washington, D.C., called Friendship Station, where the band had indeed made some friends who put us up for the night. The band had raided the medicine cabinet of our hosts and found some quality mother's little helpers, so we arrived in the Village at Folk City much less wound up than usual. Shockingly, Paul agreed to go with half-stacks, but since it was New York we still had to load everything into the venue so it wouldn't be stolen. Paul decided to play everything in a country style at first—"God Damn Job," "Hey, Good Lookin'," etc.—before building a crescendo as the pills wore off and the coke and whiskey took over.

That night, soaked and doused, I loaded our gear into the basement space of Ira and Georgia's famous Garden Street flat in Hoboken, bruising my head on the pipes and my shins on the steps. Bob also got his wish to stay with the principals of the band—he seemed concerned that band decisions would be made without him, and he always believed himself to be the leader of the band despite the obvious. He of course repaid his hosts by

rifling through their drawers and then appearing in their drawers on stage at Maxwell's.

But back to 1983. Not being the types to cry over spilled beer—considering the fact that we probably were the ones who spilled it—we drove down I-95 after the Music for Dozens showcase to Philly for a gig at the East Side Club on South Street. The East Side was a punk club for college kids, and it didn't give a rat's ass about our volume or demeanor. At that point, I was running out of money, having been living off that last paycheck from the Walker. Paul told Peter to start giving me a per diem like the rest of the group. "Where else do you wake up with a $20 bill in your pocket?" was how he put it.

Early the next afternoon, Carton and I arrived outside New York's famed Danceteria on Twenty-first Street for a showcase. A "showcase" was where they stop spinning Joy Division records long enough for you to play a set for your guest list while everyone else went to the toilets to do blow. We got there early, partly not to be late this time, partly to get a good parking space, and partly just to hang around New York. The smell of urine, trash, and street food swirled and rose above the din of sirens and horns, and I got my first real taste of New York. Upon entering the venue I found that it smelled even worse inside. The club manager walked around sticking lit incense sticks in every nook and cranny, and slowly the air became hazy and hard to breath.

After a sound check in which we purposely avoided playing much so they wouldn't tell us to turn down, we sat silently dining on the deli meats and cheese provided by the venue and patiently waited for the beer. The doors were now open, but I had to poop and these were the worst bathrooms I had ever seen, so I ventured up the elevator to the smaller bar on the third floor to see if it was any better up there. I felt leaving the venue might be a mistake—even though I had a pass, the doormen would for sure deem me unworthy of reentry. The elevator was a cramped catastrophe waiting to happen, and when I finally reached my destination I realized my mistake too late, and it was already headed back down. It was hard to tell if the upstairs toilet was any better or worse than in the main room because it was pitch black without even a reflection in the mirror. I pushed in the doors to one of the stalls and hit someone, forcing their partner to wince and me to apologize profusely as I fumbled my way out the door and hurried down the stairs avoiding the elevator.

Next up was the "other club on the Bowery," Great Guildersleeves, which was not a popular venue with the cool kids of New York, even though Johnny Thunders' Heartbreakers and the Elvis Costello and the Imposters had played there. If Folk City a few nights back had been "Music for Dozens," this one was "music for a dozen." That night we were playing with Hüsker Dü, who I watched down a tray of lukewarm deli coffee before they went onstage and then collapse in the dressing room after playing an unbelievable set for about a dozen people. The opener that night was the Young and the Useless, featuring Adam Horowitz of the Beastie Boys. If there was a time machine, I think many more people would have gone to that show despite the club's lack of cool factor. The Dean of American Rock Critics, Robert Christgau, was present in the handful of attendees, but that night I met the Dean of the Fanzine, Jack Rabid, whose zine *The Big Takeover* is like an encyclopedia of alternative music. One night on a future tour he would let me stay at his apartment, and I slept on the only bare space of floor that wasn't occupied by stacks of wax and newsprint. But I didn't care, because I stayed up with my flashlight reading cover to cover.

From there it was my first trip to Brooklyn, and when I say *trip* I mean it. We could not find this fucking place, we drove around and around for hours before we finally arrived at the hair metal venue Zappa's. Peter Buck once called R.E.M.'s show at Zappa's "the lowest point in the band's history." (Ira Kaplan once said Yo La Tengo's worst gig ever was opening for the Replacements' roadie's Alice Cooper cover band on Halloween at 7th St Entry in Minneapolis.) At Zappa's all the promo pictures on the wall were of Long Island hair metal bands that did their makeup way better than us.

Local support was called Squirm: they laughed at us like were an Archie comic. I was excited to see the headliner Flipper, as I was a big fan of their song "Sex Bomb," but we had to leave early to navigate the roads back to Jersey. I did however watch their guitarist change their fan belt in the parking lot and then followed him backstage where he restrung his guitar without wiping the grease from his hands.

Eastern Whirl, Last Shows

The bands' first booking agent was Frank Riley, who worked out of an office that could have been occupied by Philip Marlowe in New York City, and who built the coolest roster in rock and roll. I didn't really know much

about Singer Management other than its name was on the letterhead of our itineraries and that the receptionist, Randi, was very attractive and very much not interested in us at all. And the "professional" level of the Replacements seeped into everything we touched: even at the top of our itinerary of confirmed dates, it said, "...so far."

Still, I didn't care that the drives on tour zigzagged back and forth across the state of Ohio, passing towns that we would later come back to and play. Cleveland to Nashville to Detriot to Kent, Ohio, might have seemed like a lot of driving on paper. But like the song says, "I got no place else to go."

In Kent, Ohio, at Mother's—which was really just the Kent State student bar—I was told that Alice Cooper had played there at the very beginning of his career. I used that bit of information, true or not, to try and get myself onto the set list that night to sing "Eighteen." But I was never on the list. That night they had a food drive for the local food shelf, where everyone got a discounted ticket if they brought nonperishable food items. These were dropped into the traditional "barrel at the door." To be honest, the show didn't go that well and the crowd didn't get the joke. By the end of the night the remaining punters in the crowd had retrieved the donations from the barrel, some to throw at the band. It was right around then that Paul looked over to me and asked if I'd still like to come out and do "Eighteen."

The last show on the itinerary for the first tour was in Boston at the Rat in Kenmore Square. Boston is well known as a confusing city to navigate even with GPS. For us, in 1983, we would just look for the Citgo sign and keep turning toward it. The Rat itself had played host to so many cool bands it's impossible to list them. The stage was stocked with speakers and lights, and they didn't care if you turned up. The green room was pocked by holes with pipes running out of them that served as a sort of skyway for the rats to scurry over in search of an unattended grinder from the Pizza Pit next door. I'd like to tell you it was the worst bathroom I'd ever seen, but it was boarded up since it made no sense for management to continue to repair toilets that would just be kicked to pieces the next night. Upstairs in a restaurant called the Hoodoo BBQ, one time named one of America's ten best restaurants, the homeless people the owner fed out in the back lot everyday would have been inclined to agree—as would the huge herd of rats that fed on the grease. If you were lucky, a young Dicky Barrett, who would later form the Mighty Mighty Bosstones, would burst in off the street, only to have the bouncers make him throw himself out. I was told if he didn't do it with the proper menace required, they would pick him up, bring him back in, and do it properly. Flipper was hidden on the jukebox under the title of current hits. At lunchtime the cops would come in with an empty cooler and leave with it full.

Downstairs, Mitch, the manager of the Rat, was always flanked by two huge bouncers. He had a tracheotomy and talked through a pneumatic vibrator—after the show he would say in a tin voice, "You guys were just

a couple admissions short of hitting bonus." He actually warmed up to us enough to give me a case of Bud to take with us after a show, though it was too late: we had already stolen one.

As I mentioned, the Rat had a massive amount of stage lights. Paul hated lights. I would always make the light guy focus on my chest so that during the show the lights wouldn't be in Paul's eyes. Every night for eight years some concert industry professional would explain to me, in a degrading tone, how concert lighting worked, and after I was off the stage they would refocus the cans. When we took the stage, Paul would use his guitar to redirect the beams, and I would unplug every cable I could find. However, one night I put the smoke machine inside Bob's guitar cabinet, and when he played a blistering solo I flipped on the smoke. He waved the smoke away like it was a fart, at the same time patting himself on the back.

Even though Peter had added a show down the pike in Worcester, I decided to stay in Boston. Back home in Minneapolis, I was mocked by the

punkers because I aspired to be a roadie. They would (and still do) sarcastically call me "Super Roadie," but in Boston you were "crew." It was a real thing. I told Paul I thought if I stayed in Boston I could get work. He told me I already had work.

The first Replacements tour being officially over, what was there for us to do but play one more fucking show? And so the next night we played at the Xit in Worcester, Massachusetts, which was good because now we could have a "worst show of the tour." There were less than a handful of people and one paid attendee, as I recall it. Before the show Paul told me, "We're gonna play until that fucker leaves." Hours later the paid attendee was still there, and I seem to remember Paul muttering before he left the stage hours later, "Don't you have anyplace to fucking be?" Angry about the added show, I'd been sending that attendee free beers from the bar all night long.

Get Out of the Basement

After the show in the woods outside Worcester, I sat with a bottle of Jack and a twelve-pack and burned leftover construction materials from the condo development where we were staying. The band hovered inside the promoter/record store clerk's spotless abode as he and Peter swirled red and white. Carton disappeared to wash his clothes, and the band silently joined me at the fire. Or more to the point, near the Jack Daniels. Suddenly, Carton burst on the scene with the acoustic and started into some lame jam about clean clothes, and we all laughed and then Paul grabbed the guitar and went into a folk classic written by a foul-mouthed twentysomething in an age of precorrectness, and my summer at Young Life camp finally paid off with John Denver and Peter, Paul and Mary, a little Allan Sherman, and the Geezinslaw Brothers thrown in for good measure.

INTO THE LEMON JAIL

In May 1983, as an audition for a potential summer tour with R.E.M., we opened a show for them at Navy Island in St. Paul. Also on the bill were the Suburbs, who had brought Paul Stark, the president of Twin/Tone Records, to do their sound mix. Apparently, he decided to do ours as well, because just as I was finishing the setup he asked me over the P.A. to check the drums. I hit the snare as hard as I could to try and mimic Mars, and it went okay until he asked me to play a beat. *Crash slap boom boom boom.* Twenty thousand people watched the worst drum check in history. Twenty-five years later Sara Romweber,

-I'M IN TROUBLE
-Fuck School
-You LOSE
-Stuck IN the Middle
-Color Me Impressed
-Hospital
-Ace of Spades
-Job Country
-Love you till FRIDAY
-Heyday
-Favorite Thing
-Run it
-Lookin For YA
-Kids Don't Follow
-Customer/Hate Music
-Noise

Navy Island set list

the drummer from Let's Active, who also opened that show, approached me at the Cat's Cradle in Chapel Hill and told me she emulated my drum check every show after that, so I guess it had its place in history.

Although we had seemed to pass the audition, I couldn't help feeling somewhat unwelcome on tour with R.E.M. that summer. While the band seemed happy to have us along, the house crew came on a little cold. When the Replacements got big enough to play Headliners in Madison we had a broken guitar stolen off the stage, and I drove around to all the party houses on Mifflin Street until I found it. But as we moved on to the casinos and union houses on the East Coast, things didn't go so well. Tommy would constantly antagonize them with not-so-veiled rants like *Those union fuckers* and *Fuck those union fuckers*. But it was Bob who would blindly wander through rooms and unlocked doors helping himself to anything he fancied. This was not protocol.

We were at a John Lee Hooker show in Columbus, Ohio, one night and the promoter approached me and said one of my guys was in Mr. Hooker's dressing room, and would I please go and retrieve him? The backing band was already onstage playing the opening set when I walked into the dressing room and saw The Hook cowered in the corner. Bob was over at the catering table, obliviously making himself a sandwich from the deli tray. When I told him that it was not cool, and that he needed to leave, he told me, "It's okay, they put this out for us every night."

Bob and food had an interesting relationship. He would hide White Castle burgers around our hotel room and then get up and snack on them like a squirrel in the dark. I'd hear him munching and when I told him to just turn on a light and have a seat, he told me to go back to sleep—I was only dreaming. The only time Bob ever frightened me with violence was in Ann Arbor when we were staying at a local DJ and record clerk's house on an off day. Bob was helping himself to the host's food as usual and making himself a salad cutting up carrots with a large knife. While grabbing a beer I wondered out loud if he had gotten permission to eat the food, and I reached for a slice of carrot. He pinned me to the refrigerator with the knife to my chest and wondered if I had asked *his* permission.

For breakfast on the road, I liked HoJo's and the Day's Inn—two eggs on toast, some coffee, a joint in the parking lot, and I could drive forever. Back then we didn't have Whole Foods: we had truck stops and junkie delis. Not like any of us had any fucking money, but some were cheaper than others. This would materialize in different ways, like finishing someone's pancakes or omelet, or skipping out on the tip. I would take it upon myself

R.E.M.

to cover the difference between what was left and 20 percent. Which was usually about 15 percent of it.

Peter had breakfast like everything he did, well planned and a little ADD: coffee at 12 o'clock, utensils at 3, and OJ at 6, that sort of thing. Bob was The Vulture, as you might guess, and Chris and Tommy were short on the tip but for different reasons. Tommy hadn't been schooled in the matters of etiquette, and I always felt Chris wasn't so much cheap, as Paul teased him to be, but just felt the whole thing would end at any minute and he needed to save his money.

Paul would sit down and light a smoke, ask for a glass of water, and the waitress would immediately want to be his mother or his lover and have to resist combing his hair out of his eyes and cleaning the stains from his

Into the Lemon Jail

Peter Buck

clothes. Then he would order his breakfast: coffee and a Coke. They would beg him to eat something. But fingernails and cigarettes was it.

Even in the most obscure towns R.E.M. had already played half a dozen shows and had a big following and local connections, and they shared that freely with us. They took the time to watch and listen to every note of our opening sets. Michael even went out with me to breakfast in Cleveland. Most likely he just wanted breakfast and none of his crew was up yet, but he seemed to be sincerely attempting to get to know me, which made me feel more comfortable. Being R.E.M.'s choice of opener, we were treated gingerly, but clearly the rock-and-roll status quo was not happy to see us moving up the ladder.

The best part of the tour for me was after the shows. Peter Buck and

Michael Stipe, Peter Buck, and Paul Westerberg

Mike Mills seemed to have endless knowledge of the bar and party scene in every college town on the itinerary and freely showed me how to connect with the locals to find combustibles and after-hour spots, bottle shops in dry states, and party house in college towns. Trust me, this was priceless knowledge, some of which still comes in handy today.

Because we had become popular with the Beantown scene, we were able to hold our own in big rock clubs. But in places like the casinos of New Jersey and union houses in East Coast cities, our one-foot-in-the-gutter approach to these old-school and unionized eastern icons didn't go over quite as well, so I decided to stage-manage in drag. Shockingly, that didn't help.

By now I had learned how to pack for a rock tour. I didn't need food and clean underclothes. I had these things on the concert rider, and even though the small clubs seldom came through, the college gigs came through big. Add that $20 per diem, and I could travel pretty light.

Into the Lemon Jail

Opening for R.E.M., there were days off peppered throughout the itinerary, and we got bored with all the days off. We were used to playing some dive every night for $500 so we could then get to the college gig and pick up $2,500. And downtime is not a young band's friend—without load-in, sound check, show time, and load-out, we had no direction, and it almost always led to problems. So we decided to drum up some gigs of our own.

We were in the Flats section of downtown Cleveland, a longtime entertainment area that was kind of like the next day in New Orleans all the time. Sitting in Silky Sullivan's, the bar next to Peabody's DownUnder, site of the next R.E.M. show, we were talking and the bar's owner heard us grousing about all the downtime and offered us the stage at her other club. We accepted, and without the help of Internet or social media we were able to get a small crowd to this nondescript neighborhood venue. True, it was mostly due to Michael and Peter coming down for the show, thus making it mandatory for anyone who wanted to keep their job on the R.E.M. tour.

It seems we were also reprimanded for playing a show that the promoter didn't have knowledge of. There was some sort of contractual proximity clause saying that we couldn't play in the vicinity of the R.E.M. show, lest ten fans skip out of the big affair, having seen our sorry-ass circus at some college dump the night before. But the show did wonders for the band, and we came out punching the next night, partly due to the club's awesome stage and staff and the complete insanity of all Cleveland rock fans.

The next time we took a secret show, the band changed its name. We always got clean white socks and T-shirts on our concert rider, and Chris put his artistic leanings to work by making a logo for the new band BERT. As usual one could argue all day about what BERT stood for (just like *Tim*), but I doubt it was for R.E.M.'s manager Bert. When BERT played the

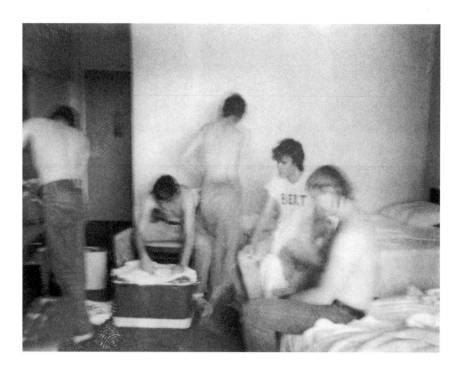

opening of a thrift shop in exchange for new cowboy shirts and stale Quaa-ludes, we put on a somewhat unbalanced performance but didn't get in trouble (with the tour at least).

R.E.M. had hired Peter as an assistant tour manager, and I believe he really thought that it was a good move, that he would learn things to help better serve the band. It wasn't. With Carton now in charge, a shadow government began to wrestle for power. Paul Stark from his lair began to try to influence events, and Peter used Carton as a puppet to tighten the budget without being the bad guy. We made a clumsy transition from sleeping on apartment floors to sleeping on hotel room floors. When we were staying with fans, we at least had options, some out-of-the-way nook where you had some privacy as the party raged on. Hold out for a shared bed, end up on the couch. After there were no roommates left, find a spot on a porch or sleep in the van with the gear. One morning in Boston I woke up sweating in the stench to the chime of church bells as I slept on the amps. Crawling out of the sliding door into the bright sun, I was greeted by lines of churchgoers in their Sunday go-to-meeting clothes. Odd that they weren't staring at me (something I had become used to), but this fine New England morning they were looking over my head at the top of old Bert. I stepped up on the pee trough and peeked at the roof to see what they were looking at. I found Chris bundled in blankets on the roof of the van, peacefully a-slumber.

As Pete and Carton tried to keep a proper tour budget that included rooms, we were typically on top of one another in a small space with little privacy and usually a subpar carpet. My favorite spot became the crack between the far bed and the wall, where you could lay cushions and pillows down into the crack and sleep under the cum-stained comforter. It was better than head to toe on the double bed, and despite the popular notion from movies, the bathtub was not only hard but a tight fit. In the day before hotel apps, Carton did his best to find budget lodgings on the outskirts of town where we could post up before or after a gig. Checking

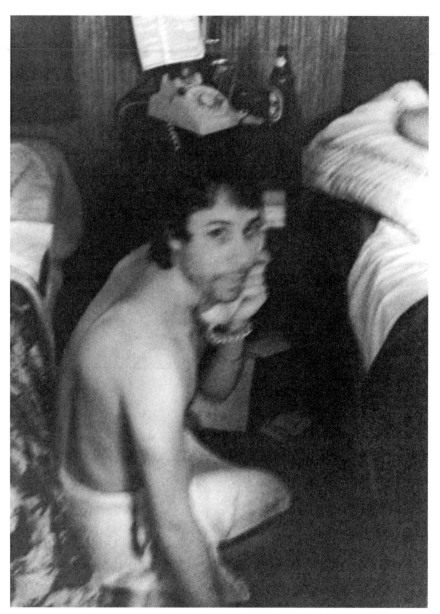

Peter Jesperson

in late the night before worked better for sneaking in the extra lodgers but had the disadvantage of checkout time coming too early with the rapid door knocks up and down the hall and the familiar screech of *Housekeeping, housekeeping.*

One night, on our way into NYC, Carton put us in a hooker hotel on Route 9 in Jersey. The woman at the desk gave us a key, and her comrade laughed and asked, "You giving them Cherry's room?" "Why not?" she said. "She won't be back." Sometime later I answered a knock at the door and found myself face to face with a couple young guidos, looking for Cherry I assumed. And apparently they did not like my answer. At the time I wore heavy eyeliner and dangling ear bobs to go with my torn and multicolored shirts, ragged jeans, and red, white, and blue cowboy boots. As they mulled over whether to kill me or not in the parking lot, I stood my ground, foolish enough to think that my ability to clear a stage would have any carryover here. Paul emerged from the room and handed out smokes, speaking low and steady into their ears, and as they turned away to a different room, I noticed the little one had a ball-peen hammer in the palm of his hand.

Getting Home, Heading West

Not too long after getting back to Minneapolis from the R.E.M. tour, I had finally gotten hired at First Ave.—not onstage, as I had hoped, but as a bar back, stocking coolers and weighing liquor bottles. I was instructed to throw away the beer bottles that had gotten rusty or nasty at the bottom of the coolers, or if the labels or caps had been ripped or damaged. I quickly worked out a system where I could stash those perfectly good—to my mind—bottles out in the parking garage to take home. And when I got busted by the club's lanky janitor, he told me my secret was safe with him. The janitor (Bob Dunlap) became an adviser to me for all things rock and roll. He somehow got advance copies of every album that dropped, and he would give me detailed reviews of everything, most of which he didn't like. I remember being surprised when he gave *Born in the U.S.A.* a thumbs-up because he really didn't like anything.

I told Bob that I had been offered a roadie job with the 'Mats on their next tour heading west. But at the same time, I was closer to my coveted stage job at First Ave. and a chance to work on the filming of *Purple Rain.* The Club—as First Ave. employees called it—was all abuzz about a new record coming out from a local artist. Seems that everyone was excited and I was no different, except they were fired up for *Purple Rain,* and the record I was excited about was *Hootenanny.*

Bob told me to "Go west, young man," that kind of opportunity comes very seldom, and that I could always come back to First Ave. And since his wife Chrissie was the booking agent, he could guarantee that.

So that fall of 1983 I climbed into the van again.

Starting out from Chicago we headed west on I-80. Only a couple of the paying gigs were four figures, and the first one at the I-Beam in San Francisco

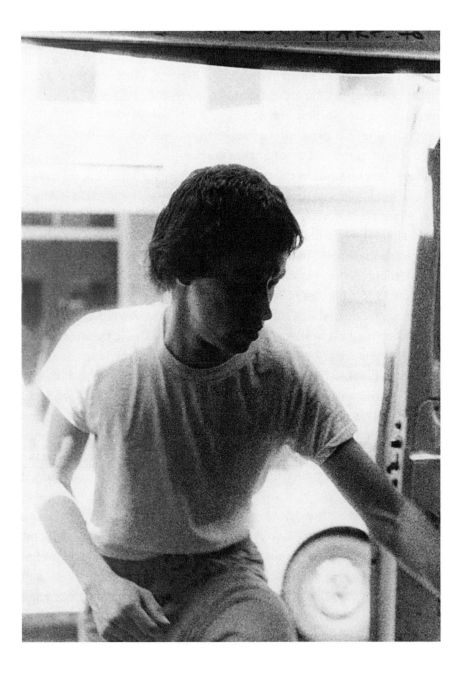

was one of those. Halfway there in the mountains of Wyoming we found ourselves in a blinding snowstorm with the tank near empty and the shrill sound of metal shearing off of our engine beneath. With only the red tail-lights of a semi to follow, I could only hope he didn't drive off a cliff, because I was sure to follow him down.

Pulling off at a gas station we found the pumps buried in drifts six feet high. I went in and told the attendant the pumps were inaccessible, and he told me there was a shovel by the door. After digging out a hose, we gassed up and were informed the only garage was up the highway in Little America, Wyoming.

Pulling into the mega truck stop I was exhausted, and I told Carton I was going to climb in the back and go to sleep while he negotiated with the mechanic. When I awoke I found Carton making a sign on a cardboard box, and he told me there was no mechanic and that he and the band were going to hitchhike while I stayed behind and got the van repaired. Groggy from sleep it all made sense to me, but as I washed up in the men's room I grew less positive. I noticed a small bearded man watching me shave, and when I looked his way he made a creepy remark about road life and asked where I was headed. He was also driving to San Francisco and had an empty RV, so I convinced him to take the band and Carton along and hurried back to tell them the good news. I hustled the gear together, guitars, snare, drums, cymbals, and stick bags and the string box, and as the stranger with the RV pulled up, I loaded the reluctant band inside. And off they went.

As it turned out the guy was so weird they jumped out in Salt Lake City and flew to SFO. For my part I went into the truck stop and had a look for a pay phone. The place was massive, with hundreds of gas pumps, several restaurants and gift shops, a barracks and grocery for the workers, and even its own post office. As I was hanging up on the tow truck driver I had found to take me back to Flaming Gorge for the needed repair, an accordion door opened up and revealed my saving grace . . . a bar.

When we'd arrive in a town on tour, I would take flyers from the club and cruise the area handing them to any young people who would take them. My promotion theory consisted of one thing: guys wanted to go where women were, and women wanted to go where guys were. The better looking the boy or girl the better chance they would sway other people. I was skinny and cute with guyliner, so I could easily slip across gender lines.

The venues were located mostly in college neighborhoods or on run-down blocks in underdeveloped parts of town. We would park behind the venue and set up a drifter camp of sorts to work from and where someone always had to stay to watch the gear. The '80s were very desperate for many people in America and our gypsy appeal was real. Guys wanted to be us and girls wanted to sleep with us, and vice versa.

Everyone had a following. Chris was dark and artistic, shy offstage. Onstage he grimaced and strained at the same time, pushing to catch up, stay ahead of, and keep the pace. With Tommy's frantic child energy he always had cougars lining up, and he toyed with them. He always had a gaggle following him, and they gave him beauty tips and products along with the adoration. Peter had record clerks enrapt, and Bob had the guitar nerds and the disenfranchised in his corner. Paul had everyone.

Me? I was the dancing monkey to the band's organ grinder. I danced and fell on the floor banging my imagined cymbals in my ragged clothes, an Oliver to the band's Dodger, who would take your watch and pawn it down the block, at the same time distractive and destructive.

At first I knew nothing of roadying. Carton showed me how to string a guitar and how to change a drumhead, but my instincts for bedlam were present from the start. Maybe it was my largely male Irish Catholic upbringing—you couldn't turn your back in my house—or just the adrenaline or trucker speed I was taking, but I could handle a crowd of punks like it was a WWE cage match.

First I would bribe them with beer before the show started, making friends with the biggest and meanest looking because in my experience those were the ones who just wanted inclusion. I would tell them how important it was that they helped me control the violence without losing the mayhem. For Paul's part he enjoyed toying with the punks. If they came to slam, he played *Stink* country-style. They knew the songs, but the beats were wrong. If the crowd was full of important scenesters and scribes, he would unleash a barrage of sound and fury that rivaled any West Coast band. The Midwest and the South were the honey holes. Less worried about their status in the local scene, the flyover crowds were uninhibited and able to go with the flow. That would allow Paul to stretch out to his full repertoire.

The monitors always sucked as far as Paul was concerned. And he wasn't wrong. Nightclub sound systems were poorly cared for and substandard from the start. That's why places like the Rat and CBGB that at least had decent gear to start with were so cool. Most places it didn't even

make sense to sound check. It only made everyone mad. They would tell the soundman to turn it down, and he would show them that he hadn't even turned it on yet. The band was unbelievably in control of their tools—they had no foot pedals or tricks. Just every knob turned full up at all times. If you handed Paul's guitar to most players, it would just scream feedback until they pulled out the cord. But in his hands it sung out sweet and powerful. This is what I learned: not how to tech but how to control the power.

After the crew got our own van to drive, we would get time to cruise around the town hitting music and hardware stores. The Replacements like any band had particular disposables like sticks and strings that were just unique enough that if we ran across any of it, we would need to buy up the whole lot. It also gave us time to tweak the performance area to our particular event, like building out stages to protect Paul without using barricades and security. The key was to let the bedlam on the other side of the

monitors build and crescendo without spilling onto the stage. The cabaret of the Replacements was never scripted, but often the same bits would be recycled at random, so the crew needed to be prepared for any eventuality.

The guitars were all destined to break. The band used no stands, had tattered cases, and put out cigarettes on the neck. No tuners in our price range would work on our stage; the needles would just bounce back and forth like a Geiger counter. Your guess was as good as anyone's if it was in tune. Instead, I learned to tune by tension and vibration—get the strings to the right slap, and with my ear pressed to the body I could feel a vibration that was close to in tune. As you can imagine, this didn't really work all that well, especially when we got to TV. I can take full blame for the discordant tuning we'd have on *SNL* (or maybe I can take the credit).

The drums were easier. The first day I took Brasso to Mars's cymbals. He walked in and poured beer and dirt on them, softly explaining to me that they sounded better dull. He would play with the thick end of

the stick, and my only issues during the show were the snare piece and the pedal chain because he broke them every night. So I just had to have spares. When the snare piece broke I'd replace the whole snare drum in the stand, and when the pedal chain snapped I replaced the whole pedal.

Tommy was his own tech. For the most part, I always felt he mocked my roadie skills, but now I realize like any teenager he was just mocking everyone. Tommy was the most expensive on a day-to-day basis: he expected brand-new round wound strings on every bass every night so that when he leapt in the air he could make those chords rumble your belly. He also had the heaviest gear. The amped SVT head and 8x10 cabinets made for lovely benches in the van, but they ruined my back early on. When we got a new soundman who didn't drink, he would taunt me by taking off his shirt and pressing Tommy's amp like a body builder. Unknown to him I didn't fucking care as long as I didn't have to lift it.

Bob's amp was Bob's amp. He didn't seem to care one way or another. But with Paul and Slim I liked to make them hot: I would turn them on hours before the show, removing the back to air them out but not use any fans to cool them. I had a box of Chinese tubes and just exchanged them at random until Paul looked happy(ish).

When the band settled on their outfits with the brightly colored coats and pants and painted shoes (I had painted shoes on tour long before them), I ordered brightly colored road cases to match each player. I had double-wide head cases, and every case and piece of gear was part of the set. The half-stacks sat on the case tops, the 8x10 case became the guitar station, and the drum trap was the rolling bar.

I was a stooge and a clown for sure, the punk rock Jerome to Paul's Morris Day, but I knew it. It was my act. I could pick up a punter and airplane spin him into a pile driver, or I could save a damsel from hapless frat

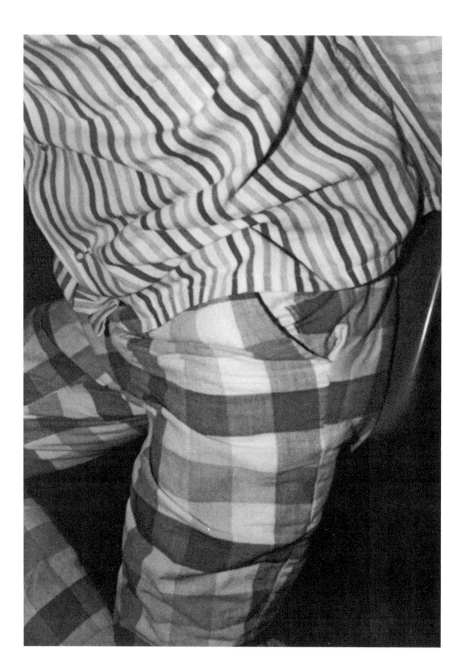

boys in the pit, all the time mixing whiskeys, chilling beers, and cutting out lines. It's true, yes: there were drugs onstage. We could make it all day (usually) clean, but eventually we needed speed to soften the blow. After a few tours I had a connect in every town. Not that I'm proud of it, or that it was even all that difficult. There was always a patsy who could hook me up, and after a while I got the feeling they were saving it up for our show so they could hang. Like Jerome, I had a mirror but for a different purpose. Sure, we used it for our manscara before the show, but when the fluff arrived I would dole it out behind the backline and then request that the band play "Wipe Out." One by one they would exchange instruments and go behind the amp for a taste. Paul went last as he always ruined the bill with his endless snot. Then he would take to the kit where I had placed the mic and kick into "Hootenanny" after some awkward reshuffling onstage.

The show would ramp up with a dose of thunder and then usually fall apart as the thunder wore off.

I could always see it in the punters' eyes. They weren't watching the band: they were watching me or looking around at security. Then they would sneak toward a weak spot in the barricade. Maybe it was closer to the stage or in a blind spot created by a cabinet. But they would always lose sight of me, and I had the freedom to be anywhere on the stage I needed to be. When they made their move, I was right there to greet them. Not that I was a tough guy. The Replacements' mosh pits were like saloon brawls in a cowboy movie, not like at Hüsker Dü, where it was closer to a Roman after-party, more pro-wrestling than the Busby Berkeley West Coast pits for the Circle Jerks or the Descendents.

When we hit the big time, I had the backline cases done up in custom colors coded to the guys' favorite suits: pink, yellow, and avocado. I had

Into the Lemon Jail

custom lowboy cases built for the Marshall heads; each one had a tray for pedals and cables. I could lay the cabinet cases down for the stacks, rolling the trays inside for quick escape. Many times my gear got dropped by stagehands as we were being rushed offstage for the headliner. With these custom cases I could plug in and box everything to be rolled off the stage right in its case.

Paul had added a Roland chorus for their new Memphis sound, as well as a 50- and a 100-watt Marshall through which he could play clean chorus or grungy through a switching box taped to the stage. Later, Slim would have his custom-built Frankenstein pedal array. It was not fixed to a board, so it was Slim's task to set up and tear down his mess in the allotted time. He was good at it since he was practically crew himself. I carefully mapped his rig over many shows. Which wasn't easy, as he was always taking broken and found electronics and adding and subtracting pedals from the mix. After some time I felt confident with his gear, and one show I set it up before he arrived. As he took off his coat, he grinned and rubbed his chin. Then he slowly bent over and, reversing two jumpers, said, "Close."

We didn't have any kind of set stage design like other bands with their backdrops and lighting plans. But one night, when we stopped for gas on our way to Newport, Kentucky, I noticed that the Kmart next door was remodeling their façade and the giant letters were sitting in the parking lot, so I stole the R and stuck it onto the truck. I hid it from the band during sound check, and after they left the stage I mounted it behind the drums and put some lights inside. When they came onstage I lit it up. Paul destroyed it with his guitar. The guitar didn't look too good either.

Another time, after a show, I stole a ten-foot all-wooden fire hydrant from the Variety Arts center in Los Angeles. On the way to our next gig I stopped at the Home Depot of the day and bought some silver garbage cans and spray adhesive. I lined the trashcans with foam rubber and created a sort of one-foot-in-the-gutter stage show, and when the band came onstage their guitars were in the bins. Somehow even though it was built pretty solidly out of thick panels of wood, Paul was able to destroy that setup as well.

At one point on tour I hired a friend of mine to be the guitar tech. He was not so much a disaster as he was just simply overmatched by the situation. I had just bought Paul a '57 Les Paul at a very nice price. On the first show of the tour he threw it at the new tech offstage. Because my friend was busy rolling a cig, the guitar's neck broke. A couple nights later he left the broken guitar in the hallway at a place called Trax—one side was a shit-kicker bar, one side a punk bar. When he returned, the guitar was gone.

    Like any good Catholic, I blamed myself and started drinking heavily. After the show I got a hold of some pills, coke, acid, and mushrooms and washed it all down with whiskey. Still sharing rooms, I began with cans of beer, throwing them at the TV. The TV itself was bolted down so I moved to throwing the furniture out the window down into the pool. All the time

screaming at everyone. I then went down to the railroad tracks behind the hotel. A few miles later I stood at the precipice of a knocked-down bridge. Sixty feet down I guessed and thought, *One more step. But first a piss.* Suddenly sober, I walked back to the hotel, lit up a joint, and all at once the mushrooms took over. Sitting in the hallway, crying, the mascara from the show running down my cheeks, I looked the scene when two kids came out of their room with snow skis. "Are you the guy who sang with the Replacements last night?" I sniffled and admitted I was. "Man, you were great!"

When I returned to the rooms, the hotel manager knocked on the door and demanded $200 or he would call the cops. Pete gave me the money, and I went to the pool to retrieve the chair I threw out the window and put it in the van for extra seating. As we drove out of town, Paul opened the side door and threw the chair onto the highway.

Have Camera Will Travel

I had always figured the fastest way to get fired was to take a lot of pictures of Paul. The others didn't really care too much. Tommy liked the camera and the camera liked him, and Chris was good for funny faces or poses—I clearly have more pictures of him than anyone else. Bob tried hard to look like a rock star onstage, and many of the Bob photos I took are the best I have. Paul didn't like light in his eyes, so subsequently his face was usually in the dark when he was onstage.

At first all I had was my dad's old Polaroid from his insurance job. Paul and I both had a "Harold" at home—both of them were salesmen. Maybe that was why he let me hang around the times I went to Paul's house, though I never really met his old man. Truth is, I never really got past the back porch or the kitchen, where his mother was always gracious and his father was just the back of a leather chair in the other room. I don't think he met mine either, yet we both attended the other's funeral.

Both the Polaroid camera and the film were vintage '70s, and they still needed the little chapstick-like shit you would rub onto the developed

picture to keep it from fading. I didn't have any, of course, so many of the photos I took with the Polaroid faded or never really turned out to begin with. My parents, however, bought me a pretty solid little 35 mm pocket camera, and that was what I used mostly on tour. I found a Kodak Disc camera in the thrift store—they were brand new in 1982 and already in the St. Vincent de Paul the next year—but it was skinny and I was able to use it at Blackberry Way during the *Let It Be* sessions. I also had a camera I got in a kids' meal at Burger King that shot 110—I called it the spy cam—and it got some clandestine photos. But all I really needed to do was point and shoot. I never really had time to think about a picture.

Like I said, taking too many photos of Paul seemed to be a bad idea. The only time I felt comfortable shooting Paul was when he was onstage, pre-occupied, and with the lights in his eyes, although during van breakdowns and the boring moments backstage, I was able to get some shots when I could tell the mood was light or no one was paying attention. Tommy often

Johnny Thunders

liked to take my camera away from me and take feet selfies. Paul did as well, but with the added risk that any time Paul took anything of yours, it was at risk of flying out the window.

Tipitina's in New Orleans had an old-school photo booth by the po'boy window, and every time we played there we took pictures that chronicled our downfall into poor health. As someone put it after viewing some shots from 1985, "I wonder what the drug of choice was on that tour."

Once they invented disposable cameras it was easier, and I'd have one or two stashed in different locations onstage, in my bag, or sitting on amps or road cases—which is where I had them the night it was rumored that Johnny Thunders might come to a show. And I didn't want to miss it if it happened.

It was July 1987, and we had sold out shows in New York City, and we'd heard Mr. Thunders was going to show up at the Beacon Theatre. Paul had me get a Les Paul Junior and a Fender Twin for him to play. I set them up the first night behind the backline on a wheeled riser so I could roll it out if he showed up, and I had the camera sitting on the amp.

When Johnny finally sauntered out onstage, he refused the guitar and grabbed the microphone. Thrown for a loop, and already breaking union rules by not using a stagehand, I pulled the rise back offstage and then grabbed the camera and was at least able to snap a couple shots from the back of the massive stage.

Basically, the fact is that when it comes to photos, I was in situations that others either ignored or were not invited into, and so I was able to get some interesting shots. Some more interesting to me than to others, some more interesting to others than to me.

Back to School

As far as myself and college, I had fled La Crosse, Wisconsin, after two years of acid trips and beer runs on Third Street, the catalyst being that trip to Madison to see the Ramones at a club called Headliners, where after getting fucked up on morning glory seeds and Michelob beer and bloodied and bruised in my first mosh pit, I had packed a bag and returned to Minneapolis to be in a band, or at least see some of the bands I had been missing. On my return to La Crosse months later I found my housemates strung out on hard drugs, at least the ones who hadn't been imprisoned from coke deals that had gone wrong at our off-campus residence.

The band didn't believe any of my stories about college, so when we were booked one night to play the VFW in La Crosse, I took them across the street to Howie's Hofbrau. On Thursday nights in college I would walk into Howie's and order a thirty-five cent beer and hand the bartender a bill with a joint tucked inside, and then all night long he would give me the "over pours" and "mistakes." When I walked in years later, he didn't even blink and only commented that it had been a while. I ordered a round of drinks and handed him a folded twenty. Suffice it to say, the band was so drunk they could hardly get onstage, let alone play, that night.

The next time I drove through La Crosse with a band it would be years later on a day off with Soul Asylum. We were on our way from St. Olaf College in Northfield to Beloit, Wisconsin, for a club date. Once again, a band was doubting the amount of stupid shit that constitute my days in college, so I pulled off the highway onto Third Street, which is a road that at one time was said to hold the world record for total number of bars on one stretch. I don't know if that was true, but every Friday my friends and I would start at the Old Style Brewery on the west side and have a drink in every bar till we reached the other end. Finding the only parking meter available, we heard a voice: "Hey, you guys are Soul Asylum, aren't you?" A young man was sweeping up outside a closed bar. We asked him how he knew that, and he said he had a poster of the band hanging up in his bar. Inside we found it to be true—the gray walls of the large bar were completely bare except one poster, and it was us.

As he was pouring us free drinks, he asked if we wanted to watch the video he took of the riots after the annual canoe race. The canoe race, I explained to the band, was when the frats all got together on the river and tried to drown their pledges (literally and figuratively). That year after the races the party had gotten out of hand downtown, and cop cars were burned and windows were broken in the melee. As we watched the fires on the TV screen, I asked the proprietor what had started the riot. As far as he could tell, his side of the street had begun to yell "Tastes great" and the other side began to shout back "Less filling."

As it turned out, I would end up visiting nearly every major college campus in America, as well as many of the directional schools. Of course, everyone knows that college radio played a large role in the rise of alternative rock—but it was the college neighborhoods themselves that played a large role in the development as well. It was fitting that the whole college scene would help give rise to the misfit fraternity that was the Replacements, not that we did any fraternal good, but we did carry on many of the timeless

traditions. Without the big paychecks that schools had for us, we may not have lasted playing all the $200 gigs in between, though hip areas in Athens, Lexington, Berkeley, Ann Arbor, and Tuscaloosa brought in good paydays as well. And it was in these towns where we felt most appreciated. On Super Bowl Sunday, in Baton Rouge, after the owner refused to pay us because of the brawl I got in with some local Cajun jocks that caused damage, the local kids broke all the windows and vandalized the place in our name. While the local LEOs were checking all the highways out of town, we were literally in their backyard getting drunk and laid.

The Chukker in Tuscaloosa was a legendary club where it was said that Hendrix shot pool and the Allman Brothers jammed and R.E.M. brought the audience out to have drinks after their show. These may have been urban legends; only the R.E.M. story was easily verified. When we arrived there in 1984, we brought a Ryder truck full of monitors and amps. The legendary Monty Lee Wilkes was our new front-of-house mixer and Casey McPherson came along to mix the monitors that we had rented to help alleviate the problems Paul was having hearing himself over the din onstage. Casey was driving the truck with all the gear, and Monty and I traded off riding with the band in the new van Peter had acquired, a Ford Econoline they called Odie, which was now completely stripped of the interior leaving only the driver and passenger seats relatively unscathed. At this point the band still had a healthy respect for not crashing the vehicle, so they left the driver seat alone. Paul spent most of his time in the passenger seat, so it too was relatively undamaged.

We had started the tour in the Pacific Northwest, so the band had flown out to Seattle and I was charged with driving Odie out from Minneapolis to Sea-Tac Airport to pick them up. Stopping in the Dakotas, I bought a tuna sandwich that proved to be inedible, so I rewrapped it and tossed it on the dash where it froze to the windshield and remained there for the duration of the drive. With the insulation and paneling torn out of the van, the cold of the western states was ripping through the now-tin-can exterior and Odie was freezing cold. To compensate for the freezing temperatures, I had blankets wrapped tightly around my legs, which made it difficult to shift the manual transmission and forced me to coast into rest areas and gas stops. Arriving in Seattle, the band clambered into the van like schoolchildren on a field trip. Bob hopped into the front seat, grabbed the tuna sandwich, and scarfed it down before I could stop him. As we drove up the 5 to Canada, he began to complain about stomach cramps and soon was retching from food poisoning. It didn't seem to affect his performance that night.

The tour wound down the coast through Los Angeles and then headed east. The band had become much more popular by now, and we always did well in the population centers of the West. But it was in Alabama at this little legendary gin mill called the Chukker when it really blew up. The place had virtually no PA system, which was not rare. Monty had been rebuilding systems all across the country in a mostly futile attempt to bring the snare and vocals above the din of the guitars. We would often end up turning the massive sidefills we brought along, using them to wash vocals over the crowd, but in Tuscaloosa we just used our gear as a house system. Backing the Ryder truck up to the stage door, Casey sat in the box with the monitor board mixing the wedges and Monty used a rigged-together mismatch of gear for the house. It was loud as fuck at sound check, but the staff at the Chukker didn't care. The show was sold out and they were going to make money.

What happened that night was legendary: hundreds of mostly young women crammed into the space and screamed like it was Cheap Trick at Budokan, completely overpowering the amps through the whole show. We had disconnected the lights to divert all the power to the PA, so there was only a single light bulb hanging over Paul. After the band finally left the stage and the crowd was all screamed out, I climbed over the amps where I was working and casually pulled the light cord, leaving only the neon beer lights shining on the walls into the dark.

College shows had perks, like a full contract rider of snacks and drinks. We began creating two separate riders, one for the clubs and one for the schools, though this could be both a curse and a blessing, such as when we opened for the Alarm at the University of Kansas. Let me start from that morning. I was thrift shopping at the downtown Lawrence Goodwill store when I came across a pair of blue-and-white striped pants, the kind the cheerleaders or rowdy fans would wear at a game in Allen Fieldhouse cheering on Danny and the Miracles. Putting them on I felt transformed, as if they were magic, and that's exactly what Paul said to me when he saw them. "Where'd ya get those magic slacks?"

But the magic quickly turned dark when at load-in the freight elevator closed on my finger and pulled it out of joint like I was always pointing west. I set it myself right there, despite the fact that the school insisted I go to the UK hospital. Rather than traditional pain moderators, I went for the bottle in front of me.

The headliners were onstage sound checking for hours—mostly the acoustic guitar, trying to get that famous signature Alarm sound in the old auditorium. The delay in our sound check only got the band drinking alongside of me, and being that it was a college show, we had a good supply of booze and a large vegetable and deli tray that was mostly ignored until we began to paste the flat meat on the walls. As the night went on, our childish behavior ramped up, and when the lights were down and the Alarm was onstage with the lead singer's foot propped up on a monitor and his acoustic guitar held high above his head in a defiant pose, we let it rip with the now-softened tomatoes.

The other perk of college shows was the legion of co-eds that we were supplied with for load-in—dozens of young women and some dudes who would use it as a way to get into the shows for free and then would try and skate out before load-out. To avoid that, we would take their college ID cards at load-in and return them after the show.

The reason the band had by this time become so vilified in the press may have stemmed from a well-placed piece of college journalism at the University of Minnesota. After some recent injuries at the Whole coffeehouse in the basement of the student union during hardcore shows (including a broken neck suffered from a stage dive off the less-than-four-foot stage), the university had banned stage diving at all campus concerts. None of the injuries had occurred during a Replacements show, and in fact the band had not played in the 150-capacity coffeehouse in years, instead drawing more than one thousand at the main hall the previous couple of shows.

But the last line of the small story that went viral in college news syndication said that the ban would be facing its first test at next week's concert featuring the Replacements. I first noticed the effect of this article in Dayton, Ohio, when we played at Wright State University. A small campus known for its diverse enrollment, there were easily as many local LEOs as students in attendance, and since it was fraternity rush week, outside the ring of campus cops around the stage was a ring of state police and Dayton sheriff's deputies ready to hold back the rowdy crowd of loners, outsiders, and disabled students.

In the South, traveling in the extreme heat, we drove with the side door of the van propped open by a 2x4, the kudzu just a blur in the stifling air, the hot tar causing a mirage of waving lines that fuzzed your vision. Any beverage remaining in the cooler was too warm to relieve your throat. For once the trough was free of garbage and urine, and we would hold on to Paul's belt as he peed out the door, the warm wind blowing it onto the side panel. At night we would sleep on the floor, one arm draped over whoever was lying next to you, for fear that one good bump in the road would send them tumbling out the door.

Driving between gigs one day on a rural route somewhere near the Ozarks, Bob is already drunk and passed out. Giggling to myself, I tie the metal ammo box that we fancied for transporting spare strings and picks to his shoelaces. Stopping for fuel, everyone piles out except a passed-out Bob. Carton pumps the gas while Paul has a cigarette and wanders aimlessly as if he is thinking of abandoning us. As I head for the small store that passes for a truck stop, Peter beelines for the pay phone, most likely to make an apology or an explanation for the night before or warning the next venue of our impending tardiness. I pass a couple of good ol' boys on the stoop, spitting and whittling. Tommy emerges from the van wearing only bright-colored highwater pants supported by Steve Urkel multicolored suspenders over his pale white shirtless body. A stolen white hotel towel is tied around his head like a turban and a green facial mask protects his face from the ravages of the southern exposure. He creeps by in his Doc Martens, causing one of the hillbillies to ask, "Who's yer girlfriend?" Before the moment can become tense, Bob shuffles through like the Frankenstein monster, his eyes half-mast, what's left of his blond hair sticking up in a glorious male-pattern bedhead, and the ammo box dragging behind him on the floor. He uses the toilet, heats up a burrito, cracks open a cold tallboy from the cooler, and then walks out of the store with no indication that he has paid for anything. Carton meanwhile settles up and we pile into the van, pulling up to the phone booth and urging the manager to hang up and join us. At this point, we're all possibly thinking to ourselves that desertion may be the better part of valor, or that *Deliverance* was a better film to view than to experience.

Driving to Memphis on another tour, Bert broke down. Something to do with the "Mark Farner Unit," as Karl from Soul Asylum would later call all engine parts. In these situations I would turn to Mars and ask him if he could fix it, and he would say, "I'll need a hammer." Hot Tennessee sun in a dry Tennessee county. In our home state we would have had Samaritans up the wazoo despite our looks, but here the roads were clogged with semis

Into the Lemon Jail

that sizzled by shaking ol' Bert and forcing us over the guardrail where we sat in the grass while the band took turns with the acoustic.

The day dragged on and morale began to slip. Then I remembered that Danny Amis, from the legendary Minneapolis surf band the Overtones, had given me a jar of moonshine while we were in Nashville. "Don't drink it straight," he told me. "You might go blind." We did.

Did You See Dere Rapids?

Whenever someone brings up Cedar Rapids, Iowa, I have two reactions. The first is to tell my Mom's old joke: "Did you see dere Rapids?" The other is to tell the story of the Replacements' visit.

We were traveling on the wings of *Hootenanny* and had a full contingent of Warner Bros. reps handling the band in each region. The handler assigned to Iowa was from Minneapolis and was a friend of Paul's. The local newspaper in Cedar Rapids had done a top-of-the-fold story in the variety section on the band and their tendency to get drunk, do drugs, and cause trouble wherever they went. The writer had taken great care to mine every dastardly deed ever blamed or claimed by the 'Mats and had in turn created quite a stir around our visit.

The local police had a couple of plainclothes guys embedded in the union crew. Of course, our pals from the local promoter's group pointed them out, and we were able to keep them isolated by assigning them jobs away from the backstage area whenever the band was around. The show of force overall was impressive, and the local LEOs seemed determined to catch us at our shenanigans after the show. I loaded out as usual but was careful to keep the undercover crew in the back of the truck where they couldn't spy on the group and their entourage—as they all the while carried on in the usual fashion that they had become famous for.

After the trucks were loaded, I pulled the tour bus up to the front of the pizza place where the label rep had taken the band after the show for a meet and greet. When I went inside I found a rather docile party of partiers anxious to split, so I grabbed a swallow of beer right out of the pitcher and a couple of slices, and we were off to the hotel just around the corner. The driver was irate with the band being the last show on the tour, so rather than circling the block to get us in front of the lobby door, he pulled up across the street, and everyone scurried off like rats jumping out of the ocean onto a sinking ship. The band went around the back of the bus, but the label rep went around the front and was run down like a school kid by a speeding driver. As the paramedics rushed him to the hospital, where he would turn out to be fine, the police were occupied with the driver. I was able to gather up any incriminating substance that I assumed would once again turn the blame toward us. Then after everything calmed down and the bus was on its way to Minneapolis, I had a raging party in my hotel room.

Firewood

The band, and especially Paul, refused to use guitar stands. "First, it's guitar stands," he'd say, "and next thing you know, you have backup singers." So I would have to try different ways to keep the guitars upright. I could always hand Paul his guitar as he went onstage, but he was resistant to that as well—plus there were still two more guys who played guitars. Also, that didn't really solve the problem of when he would lean it against the amp before he *left* the stage.

I tried making duct tape barriers on the floor in front of the amps, a kind of ridge that I would build by folding the tape, which would hopefully stop the guitar from sliding down the face of the speaker by catching the body. I even bought garbage cans that I lined with 3M adhesive and foam so the band could "throw their axe away" at the end of the set. Tommy liked them, Bob peed in his, and Paul said, "Maybe if they were used cans full of garbage."

Finally, one night in Atlanta, I had to climb into the pit to control an unusually unruly crowd who kept pushing the monitors into the base of the mic stand, knocking the microphone into Paul's teeth. I posted up in

front of Paul and took the hits from behind all night to keep him safe. After the last song I was tangled up in the skankers and watched helplessly from the floor as Paul leaned his Gibson ES335 against the Marshall and walked away. The 335 slid slowly down the face of the amp and fell to the ground, breaking off the neck. Paul turned, picked up the neck, and nonchalantly tossed it into the crowd. Paul often broke guitars for little to no reason, but this guitar called "Firewood"—so named because of the sticker on the front—was his favorite. I fought in vain with the crowd to get to it first, but they tore it apart like badgers before I could reach it. After the crowd had cleared, I shuffled around the littered dance floor kicking cans and butts looking for any pieces that might remain of Firewood but only uncovered this photo of Paul and Tommy that a photographer had tried in vain to hand up to the band during the show.

Into the Lemon Jail

Eventually, I became the one who was in charge of sticks and strings, backline and repairs. Back in Minneapolis I found out that the repair shops and music stores didn't want to take me, or for that matter, the Replacements, too seriously. On instinct one day I stopped into a small shop on South Lyndale run by a luthier named Roger Benedict. After I explained to him that the band had a tendency to trash their gear onstage most nights and there was nothing that could be done about that, I told him that I would buy all my consumables from him—sticks, strings, picks, etc.—and in turn, he agreed to do his best with the pieces of guitar I brought back from each tour.

Roger was a very chill and quiet cat who had no time for who was in the scene or was passing judgment on the band's behavior. Never once did he give me grief about the state in which the guitars returned. He just took them into the basement and returned them to me in working order.

Only once did Roger sell me a guitar that he thought Paul would like, giving me a great deal on a 1950s Gibson Les Paul Custom Black Beauty—the one that Paul broke on the very first night of the tour—and we hauled it around for weeks after, until someone stole it from backstage in Virginia. Roger also repaired a Firebird that Bob had snapped in half, and when I surprised Bob with it during a show in Duluth, he looked at me and smiled before he smashed it on the stage and handing it back to me said, "See if you can fix it now."

In exchange for Roger's work, I bought thousands of sticks and bass strings from him. He special-ordered Promark 2B oak sticks for me even though he carried no drum supplies, as well as Tommy's Rotosound strings and Fender heavy picks, Paul's GHS 10-46 round wound strings and the .73 Dunlop nylon picks he liked, which were difficult to find in other locations. You could string Bob's guitar with barbed wire and hand him a quarter and he would be happy. Roger had to special-order Slim's thumb picks. On the road I would routinely clean music stores out of Paul's and Slim's picks, even when we'd switched to a larger supplier after we lost Roger far too soon.

Sometimes the Shows Are Just a Blur

Madison, Wisconsin, Club De Wash, 1983. Everyone was broke and pissy, and we are way too loud for this tiny little lounge on the far end of State Street, and before long Paul says, "Fuck it . . . Jazz set!" They play two new songs that night: "Music Is My Life," a discordant ode to life on the road, and "Where's Our Money? Pete You're Fired." Not sure what that one was about.

New Haven, Connecticut, Toad's Place, 1983. We opened for R.E.M. at the famous club where the Stones were known to open their tours with a secret show. The back of a Toad's T-shirt lists every band you ever heard of, and even though they didn't know who we were, we were treated okay and got to play our set at our volume. This place knew that one band's opener was one day their headliner. And we were there several times after; I even shot the Soul Asylum video for "Misery" there. I liked those guys so much.

Raleigh, North Carolina, The Pier, 1983. Somehow, our booking agent Frank got us on as the opening act for the popular Violent Femmes. Each night their fans had to withstand a 120-decibel wall of sound from the Replacements or give up their spot in front of the stage. The band played killer versions of '70s hits, like "Love Grows (Where My Rosemary Goes)" and "Temptation Eyes," along with their originals to a captive audience. Before the show that night I had to drive to Chapel Hill for hard liquor because Raleigh was a dry community other than beer and wine, so I asked the Femmes if they wanted me to pick something up for them. The bass player smirked at me and asked for Pernod, "If you know what that is." When I got back I left a brown bag with a mason jar of Corn Squeezins in their dressing room with a note: "This is the closest they had."

Houston, Texas, Fitzgerald's, August 1, 1983. Hot. Fitzgerald's has a nice big concert room, but we played in the downstairs bar in a very small room with an even smaller crowd and in front of a fish tank. The people there were not fans, just people who were drinking, and there was a lot of back and forth between the band and a couple of fellas in particular. The band actually tried to keep it cool by playing many of their requests for covers by Skynard and Hank; it's not like they didn't know them anyway. Eventually, it got ugly like it usually does, and the tank broke, spilling fish and shells all over the floor. Years later we played a converted bank in downtown Houston, and behind that stage they had an aquarium that housed a twenty-foot boa constrictor. Halfway through the show the vibrations from our volume had bounced the brick holding the top on the aquarium loose, and the snake had had enough and forced its way out through the sheetrock, craning its body toward Mars. I went behind the drumkit and took hold of its head trying to force it back into its home. But it was one strong-ass muscle of love. Soon two giant bouncers were in the room behind the stage trying to pull it back inside while I pushed from the stage, Mars looking nervously back as he leaned forward over his kit and continued to play.

A VFW in Kansas City, Missouri, 1983. We're on a bill with Dave Grohl's band, Scream, a punk marathon that was clearly oversold and undermanaged. After our set I insisted on running all our gear out to the van where I sat in the parking lot viewing the affair from what I considered to be a safe distance from the impending carnage. As I sat in the warm sun drinking warm beers, I saw the windows of the old building begin to break out from the inside. One by one they popped and crashed two floors to the tarmac, and I soon realized that the punks weren't kicking them out, for once, but the sheer volume of bodies in the un–air-conditioned hall was forcing the windows to blow. Soon the bodies were being hauled out one at a time, carried by arms and ankles, others fireman style, all of them with their lips turning blue and their expressions more blank than usual. The band had joined me by now, and when the manager came down, having been paid, I suggested we leave before the emergency crews blocked the exits.

Ann Arbor, Michigan, Joe's Star Lounge. The clerk from the local record shop Schoolkids Records let us stay at her house for a few days since we had some off time. This is when I confronted Bob about eating the food in the fridge and he put the knife he was cutting carrots with to my throat. I

pulled Paul aside at one point and asked him what was up, since this was the first time Paul was actively involved in finding us a place to crash, so I was a little suspicious. I said to him, "I didn't think that girl liked any of us." "She doesn't," he replied. They got married a few years later.

Cleveland, Ohio, the Pop Shop, 1984. The soundboard was in the hull of a dry-docked boat in the middle of the room. We stayed at the Comfort Inn that was once famous as *the* rock hotel of all time. Swingos is where Elvis once bought out all the rooms with a suitcase full of cash and Keith Moon pulled one of his most famous pranks, when he entered the lobby dressed as a cop and handcuffed groupies to his wrists. For his part, Bob took a shit in the ice bucket then sent it down the elevator.

California

Of all the towns the band had strange relationships with, Davis, California, was one. Our first time there on that fall '83 West Coast swing we played a house at 616 Anderson Road. Sometimes referred to as the Pirate House,

Into the Lemon Jail

616 was off-campus housing not too different from what I was used to. The difference was that 616 promoted punk shows—the Meat Puppets and Violent Femmes were two of the more prominent groups to have played there. Not really being the type to pay attention to the manager, I had no idea it was a house party we would be playing, and the unassuming rambler gave me some pause as we pulled into the driveway like in-laws on a holiday. Setting up in the living room with a keg nearby and a poolside bar, it actually wasn't much different from any show in Lori Barbero's basement, minus the pool and the pond. That night at 616 wasn't one of the best shows we had, but with no stage for me to secure I spent the night mingling with the crowd and enjoyed the keg like a frat boy.

By our next visit to Davis we had moved up to the lounge in the student union on campus. It was not much different from a living room in a party house. The bar was in a nearby building and that's where I was when a kid from my old neighborhood in Minneapolis approached me, telling me that he was now "farming" in the hills. He had planted in a truck bed and would drive it to different locations to avoid the police. He spent most of his time sitting in the cab listening to the scanner. My buddy was famous in southwest Minneapolis for his ability to find and/or create trouble, and he once told me I owed him big for not telling the police that I had burned down a neighbor's garage. I insisted that I hadn't been involved and he agreed. But his point was that he still could have *told* them I did it.

At show time Peter was beside himself. The band was upstairs trashing the dressing room and refusing to come onstage, and Peter wanted me to go up and see what I could do about it. The green room that night was a conference room with expensive wood panels and gilded frames of the campus elite. As I entered a bottle of beer crashed against the wall high and inside, the band now playing a spirited game of beer bottle baseball, a simple game the band had invented that only required two cases of bottled beer. First, you simply place the cases at either side of the room. Next, the "pitcher" takes an unopened bottle of beer and pitches it at the "batter," who has a full and unopened bottle by the neck like a bat. When I say *at*, I mean that the pitcher's object is not to throw a strike but actually to bean the batter. The batter for his part is not trying to get a hit. He is trying to defend his skull from the oncoming object. The result, nearly every time, was two broken bottles spraying glass and suds all over everyone. If it's a ball, it usually breaks on the wall.

Tonight, however, the hardwood furnishing was only dented in and the bottle was retrieved for another game. By breaking up the game between Tommy and Paul, I had turned their attention to Chris, so they held him down and forced whiskey down his throat like you might feed a baby giraffe. I finally convinced them to head to the stage and mentioned to Peter he might try and get the check before anyone went inside.

They were too drunk to even finish a song. Chris fell off the drum throne, slipped between the stage and the back wall, and was unable to extricate himself even with my help. Just because tonight sucked didn't mean we wouldn't be needing working gear tomorrow, so I began to break down the backline during the show to keep Paul from breaking everything. While I was stacking it near the exit, the situation out front had gotten ugly—the house lights had been turned on and the PA turned off. By this time Bob was long gone and Tommy was snickering at the carnage. Chris was still on the floor behind the stage and Paul had begun to sing a capella showtunes to a crowd that was now turning both parties belligerent. I had taken away Paul's guitar, and the mic was cold, but that wasn't stopping him from belting out "Hello, Dolly!"

As I continued packing the backline, my old neighbor reappeared in the doorway. He was now in full camouflage and he told me he had picked up some chatter about us on the scanner. I went to get the guys and he helped finish packing the backline. When I got everyone in the van, my friend directed me across the campus green space and out a service road that led straight to the highway out of town, and we disappeared into the night. Heading down the highway toward LA, we were happily out of reach of the Davis police when Paul leaned over the driver seat, handed me a scrap of paper, and said, "Hey, Spilly, I wanna go to this party."

Azusa, California

The wind was whipping up the sand so hard it was getting in my eyes and blinding me while I tried to load in. The staff was surly and mean—the entire venue clearly unhappy we were even there. The venue manager came down on Tommy the hardest because he was under eighteen, telling us he would need to sit in a locked room after sound check until show time. There was a two-drink minimum for those of drinking age and a surcharge on any tickets bought by the underage, who had to stay in a roped-off area away from the stage.

While I was enjoying a steak before the show, Paul asked if I thought I could load out without the bar staff noticing. I told him there was a stage door behind the drums and if we waited until the openers went on, I could most likely pull it off in fifteen minutes. I packed up the guitars and cables while the stage was dark, positioned everything by the stage door, and pulled the trailer up outside. When the openers began their set, I started throwing it all in the trailer as fast as I could while Paul rounded up everyone else. In less than fifteen minutes we were kicking up gravel as the bouncers chased us through the parking lot.

Hightailing it west to LA, we looked over the weekly rag and spotted a show at the Lingerie that would suit us. Thelonious Monster was headlining and Bob Forrest was happy to let us play. As he was walking me through the club, I saw an older gentleman who looked a lot like Doctor Seuss. When I commented on the resemblance, I was told that his nephew was in the opening band. There were no cell phones or Internet in those days, but somehow without a tweet or a post most of the fans from Azusa showed up.

On another tour out west we played at the famous Roxy in LA. I went next door to the Rainbow Bar to look for Slash or someone from Poison and

have one of their famous $5 cheese sand-
wiches and, in general, look for rock stars.
Lemmy wasn't there, so I ate my sandwich
at his video poker game. When I returned to
the Roxy, management was frantic because
they couldn't find Paul anywhere. I had work
to do onstage but told them that if he wasn't
back soon, I'd look for him. I handed Mars
his sticks, toilet paper, and duct tape after
breaking the tips off the sticks so he could
wrap them into a grip for the show.

As I turned to leave, Chris grabbed my
arm and pulled me close. Slipping a handful
of small glass vials into my hand, he whispered that I should throw them under the
punters' feet during the show. Even though
I knew better I asked him what they were.
"Morning Breeze," he told me, a joke store
item sold as fart smell, but it really smelled
like rotten eggs. In fact, it was the same shit
people mixed with gas to detect leaks.

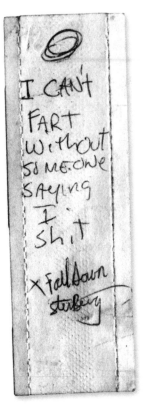

Paul "Falldownsterberg"

Out on the street the crowds had gathered with the usual hangers-on,
and a look-alike for Peter Criss was doing well with the tourists. I looked
east past the club, looking for Paul, but nothing stood out. I walked up to
the liquor store under the Angelyne billboard where years ago I had first
spotted Fabio (we'd seemed to run into him every trip since). Fabio wasn't
there, and neither was Paul.

Across Sunset from that corner was a fancy bistro. It was also the nearest
bar from there. I slipped past the valet, and despite my painted boots and
waxy hair the maître d' greeted me warmly and asked if I was looking for my
friend. He brought me to a bar in back where I found Paul sitting with his own

Into the Lemon Jail

bartender and drinking a scotch. Paul introduced me as Spilly and ordered me a bourbon. The barkeep poured me a tall one and, smiling, handed me an extra linen napkin. I took a big drink and we sat quietly for a few minutes, and then I asked Paul how the food was. "Food?" he said, and we laughed and before he could order another, I told him that everyone was worried and they were hoping he would go onstage. He sighed and said he would.

We downed our drinks and started to head back, and before I left, I tossed a couple of the vials Chris had given me onto the floor.

So at encore time Mars, who had been looking over at me and motioning toward the crowd all night, was getting a little upset that I wasn't going through with the bit. To be honest, I was worried about a stampede of mass panic, even then, long before today's troubles.

I was about to relent when the Thelonious Monster front man stuck his head through the side curtain and asked if I needed anything. Handing him the remaining vials, I told him to roll them out under the skankers' boots. A few minutes later the crowd cleared the room. Paul looked at Mars, who was laughing his ass off, and then at me, who wasn't. And then he walked off the stage.

Back to Boston

Kenmore Square was the center point of our trips to Boston. Besides the Rat and the Pita Pit next door, Store 24 was where we got our combustibles and Howard Johnson's was where we would stay even when we moved on to the larger venue the Paradise down the road toward the colleges. But it didn't matter to me. I usually stayed out so late I just climbed on the bus in the early morning, leaving notice for the driver that I was in my bunk. I would sweat or freeze until the driver saw the note and mercifully started the generator. Then I would sleep peacefully until load-in.

Across the fens just past Fenway Park was Store 54, a thrift shop of sorts. To call it a thrift shop is almost an insult, except that it was a hell of a thrift shop, as well as a hub of art, music, photography, and culture. The proprietor would against his better judgement let me sleep on the for-sale furniture and had an army of punks, squatters, and homeless that would scour the alleys behind the student apartments around Kenmore and BU in general. They would bring him boxes and bags of clothes and household items that students would take the time to fold and box before discarding on their way out of town or on their move to a more affluent neighborhood. The payment would vary from snacks and change to trinkets or scarves from the store's inventory. The two coolest items I witnessed being brought in was a dentist chair shaped like a gaping set of teeth with an unfurled tongue for a seat and an eight-foot stuffed bear on casters posed in a menacing position.

It was hot in Boston the summer of '84, and the brownstones in Boylston absorbed and radiated the heat like a pizza stone. Humidity clung tightly to my throat like the ill-fitting turtlenecks I wore in high school to hide hickeys. We had played in Cambridge the night before, all going our own ways after the show. For my part I had found refuge on the couch of a girl I knew. With no AC, I had stripped to my skivvies and sweated my ass off on the couch's rough cushions until early the next morning, hungover, I felt a slap on my sweat-soaked boxers and opened my eyes to an older man wearing a dark mustache and tighty whiteys. He told me to scootch down the coach, where he sat silently next to me for several minutes and concentrated on rolling a large joint. He wet the finished product by sliding in into his mouth and dried it with the flame from a Bic disposable lighter. Then, sitting back, he inhaled deeply and spoke.

"So I'm told you're in a band," he half-asked, clearly with no intention of sharing his joint.

"I'm a roadie" was my reply.

"A roadie!" he laughed. "Hell, I like roadies," he said and handed me the joint. "This will cool you down," he said.

Into the Lemon Jail

The roommate's daughter was now awake in the next room. She was all of nine and had on a porkpie hat and rubber vacuum belts for bracelets. Putting on MTV, she sang along to "Girls Just Wanna Have Fun" like she was onstage herself. The mustachioed man slapped me on my sweaty knee and told me to get dressed, and the ladies emerged from their rooms and handed me some orange juice.

The mustache man was right, the weed did cool me down. It was also some of the strongest I'd ever had. He reemerged from the bedroom dressed to the nines, gave me a wink under his stingy brim hat, and slipped out the door. After he left, I asked my friend who he was, and she told me he was the bass player in the J. Geils Band.

Playing on Lansdowne Street in Boston on another tour we parked our bus across from the Green Monster. I came out after sound check to find Paul and Abbie Hoffman's son in conversation in the front lounge. I sat down with them and learned about the plan to put free food trucks on the street that, even when closed, would still supply hot coffee through spigots on the outside because "homeless people always seem to have coffee cups," said Hoffman's son. He also said how the government was following him constantly in order to get his father's address book. "You wouldn't believe the phone numbers," he said. "Che Guevara is in there." He had become so concerned that he even had mirrors installed on the inside of his sunglasses frames so he could see who was following him.

After he left, I remarked to Paul that he was one paranoid cat. To that, Paul produced the aforementioned spy shades that he had taken off the table. Putting them on, he laughed and said, "More so now."

X

On the X tour in the fall of 1984 we were confronted with the biggest problem we would face in the coming years—seated venues. Paul had taken to bringing a chair onstage and trying to coax the aging punks to stand up during our set. Of course, between Paul and the crowd were a dozen blaze-orange–wearing pumpkin-armed bouncers tasked at keeping the punks in the rows and out of the tiles.

One night in southern California, the headliner's drummer, D. J. Bonebrake, decided to help me get the band chairs and even brought one onstage himself to watch the set. It didn't do anything to loosen up the scene for our set, but when X hit the stage the place broke down and the crowd went berserk. I saw a punter reach out and grab at Exene's leg, and then John reached out and kicked the guy right in the mouth. After the show I approached John about the incident, and he wondered if I thought he had gone too far. "No," I said. "I was just wondering where I can get some shoes like that."

That Thanksgiving, John and Exene invited us to their house. We arrived to all the trimmings of a proper moveable feast—Wild Turkey and Top Jimmy. Top Jimmy was the guy in LA that the indie rock scene could trace their roots back to. Every town had a guy like this, the guy who had cover bands in the '60s and '70s that played at the school dances and proms while cutting their teeth in the club scene with the older cats. Curtiss A was a good example in Minneapolis, and Paul and I would always try and identify the Curtiss A of each town. Top Jimmy was the Curtiss A of LA, and his band, the Rhythm Cats, featuring Carlos Guitarlos (the Slim of LA?), opened for us when we played the legendary Al's Bar.

After shows on the X tour we'd go out and have some fun. We weren't used to having hotels like this every night, and we enjoyed some popularity as the up-and-comers supporting punk legends. One night John decided to come with us to the party house—every town had one or two party houses that no matter who lived there, year after year, it was the house that had the parties after the shows. So John came with us and all went well for a while; the hosts were even flattered that we'd brought him. But as it is with any gunslinger, there is always some punk that wants to bring him down, and sure enough as the night got long someone crossed John's path.

JOHN: *What are you looking at?*
PUNK: *Nothin', absolutely nothin'.*
JOHN: *Excuse me?*
PUNK: *You heard me.*

At that, John shot out of the prone position on the couch and took the guy down the front stairs with Paul on his back like Yukon Cornelius. John's roadie told me to gather the flocks, and as we went past the carnage he grabbed his singer and I grabbed mine, and we split that scene.

Scorgies

Scorgies was one of those clubs that was built for hard rock and metal, with its five-foot plywood "wall of death" in front of the stage to keep the punters off, all the way down to the adjoining strip club next door. The staff there seemed to treat every show and every band the same. It was a good venue that brought in a good crowd of regulars that added to your own turnout.

Driving overnight for a show at Scorgies in August 1985 I found myself the only one awake as I cruised east through upstate New York on the turnpike. Even Paul had crawled into the back and for once wasn't sitting next to me changing the music and pounding heaters. I took this rare opportunity to smoke a little weed and put on my Tom Waits tape that I had hidden from Paul during the Great West Coast Tape Purge of '84. As the sun slowly rose in the distance I was one with the world until I felt the van begin to lurch. I looked down at the gauges and immediately saw the issue. I was out of gas. I pulled over with the blood rushing to my head. How could I have been so stupid? We were on the turnpike, miles in either direction to a plaza. I had noticed an exit two miles back and the sign mentioned a town, so I wrote a note to the band and crossed the empty highway, jumping the fence on the westbound lane and headed through the woods.

Soon I was forced to wade a small marsh and hop some homeowner's redwood fence, only to be chased by an angry dog, dodging slides and a sandbox. I hurdled a chain-link fence like I did when the cops chased us through South Minneapolis (I did hold the 330 hurdle record in high school).

I avoid the town's Barney Fife and find Goobers Fillin' Station on the main road. I borrow a can and fill it up, taking a couple huffs for good measure. Inside, the clerk tells me he'll need my driver's license or a $5 deposit on the can. I toss him a five, thinking that I'll never return it but maybe the band will pee in this for a while instead of the van's doorstep.

Heading back I take the street this time and put out my thumb. The first car to come by in the early fog pulls over and picks me up. Inside was a scraggy-ass dude with a backseat full of items: clearly he was an extreme hoarder or possibly lived in his car. He offers to drive me to the van for $10. I tell him I only have $5, but he can have the gas can and return it to the station for another $5. Turning onto the turnpike he asks me if I cut through the woods to get to town. I tell him I indeed had and he says, "Didjya get chased by that damn dog?"

About a half-mile from the van I see a solitary man walking with not so much a limp but more a painful shuffle. "One of yourn?" asks the driver. I ask him to slow down.

There is not any room in the car for Paul, so I just wave him back to the van as we roll by at a reduced speed. He acknowledges me and turns slowly with his signature limp, and I look back at him in the sideview mirror that says "Objects may be closer than they appear," thinking to myself, "I doubt it." Paul would never trust sleeping in the van again. The hoarder took one look at my gang and drove off without the can. Not wanting the smell in our van (even though it might be an upgrade), and figuring flammable vapors around this crew could only be trouble, I toss the empty tin into the brush.

Paul arrives soon after, gets in beside me, and asks, "Did you buy any smokes?" I shake my hair no and he mumbles something about how I never buy any smokes.

A Not-So-Great Use of Paint

The 688 in Atlanta is a club so storied that Iggy Pop's set list was actually painted on the stage wall. That was the night Chris got the idea that instead of writing graffiti on the walls of the clubs, we would bring house paint and cover up all the graffiti and beautify the green rooms of the venues we played in. So he started to collect cans of paint from the storage closets of any venue where he could find it.

That night at the 688, Paul and Bob had a different approach, and during the set they got into one of their patented "tussles" that ended up with Bob throwing Paul through the sheetrock and destroying the sacred Iggy Pop set list. I truly had never seen a venue manager more bummed out than that night.

Of course, Chris never used the cans of paint for good, but he continued to take them whenever he could and save them in the tour vehicle. It was those cans of latex that would later reappear on a trip from Toronto to Cleveland.

Driving to the border in a rented RV on our way to Cleveland, the band got so drunk on Canadian beer that Peter waved Monty and me to the side of the road. He came to the window and, looking completely disjointed, asked me if I would please trade places with him and drive the band. They had gone too far and he just couldn't take it anymore.

"How bad could it be?" I thought to myself and agreed to take over the RV.

When I got in, I saw four grinning maniacs and piles of lumber and foam torn from the seat cushions and twisted metal with cans of house paint thrown everywhere. I drove toward the U.S. border, and the band resumed the chaos, lighting things on fire and pulling out the toilet, splashing urine and the blue fluid that was meant to control the smell everywhere, then starting a bonfire of their vanity. Mars finally put the paint to good use by tossing it on the fire and his bandmates, extinguishing the

flames while Bob reached up and put his hands over my eyes as I drove down the highway.

My reaction was to take my hands off the wheel and spread them to heaven. Then pushing the gas to the floor, I shouted, *If this is what you want, ye sinners, this is what ye get!* in my best Father O'Ruckus voice. Paul jumped on Bob and struggled with him to get his hands off my eyes. Seems as if Paul was not quite ready to go.

I drove into the border station, now covered in house paint myself, and we were quickly ushered into a search bay. The border agent asked me for our passports, but I only had my own; Peter had kept the band's passports in his briefcase, and he and Monty had already passed through into America. The band was ordered out of the RV and into a holding room. The border agent angrily approached the RV door, asking me if we had any contraband. I told him that there was nothing illegal inside, but that I highly recommended that he not enter the vehicle as it was not a sight for the weak of heart. That seemed a challenge to him, so he went inside,

quickly reemerging with house paint on his crisp clean boarder guard uniform. "What the hell's this?!" he seethed. "Who do these assholes think they are, the fucking Who?"

"One does," I replied. "The others are split between The Clash, the Pistols, and Salvador Dali."

"Here's the deal," he hissed. "You get these assholes out of here, and if you ever cross my border again, it will be hell to pay."

I gathered up my giggling flock and drove on to Cleveland. After dropping them at the hotel, I took the RV down to the Cuyahoga banks and parked it under a bridge where crackheads were known to gather. I left the keys inside and the doors unlocked, but alas, it was still there in the morning.

CBGB

When we finally got a show at CBGB, we were the opening band. What I didn't realize was that opener, or support, at CB's was actually the slot after

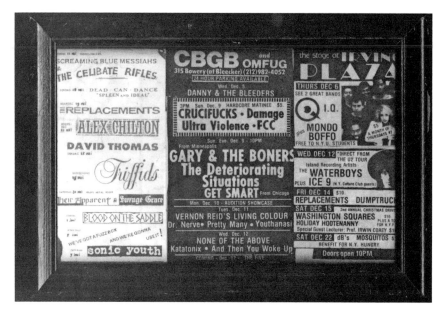

At CBGB as Gary & the Boners

the headlining bands. The early slot was reserved for a pay-to-play band that, in order to secure the slot, was required to bring down a busload of presold admissions. After that, the main bands of the evening would play and then at around 1:00 or 2:00 a.m., the support band would play to fill out the evening.

The buzz from our appearances around town, and it being New York City, was strong enough to keep label reps, lawyers, and ex-patriots from Minnesota up late enough to come to the show. It was relatively successful, mostly due to the larger sound system and the fact that CB's was in no condition for us to do any (further) damage. At a later show at CB's, as we loaded the trailer, the NYPD meat wagon pulled up and loaded in a dead junkie from the flophouse upstairs.

After the show, we pulled away and began heading uptown. Tommy and I were in the back, sort of like kids on a family vacation, when we

Into the Lemon Jail

noticed the trailer was no longer following the van. We shouted for Carton to stop, and I jumped out of the back and started chasing down the now-wayward U-Haul, with no clear plan of what to do when I caught it.

It was careening toward a group of yellow cabs standing at the curb, and I tried to direct it back into the street. I had no chance as it knocked me aside and crashed into an empty cab. By this time Carton had swung around and pulled up next to it: he hopped out and we grabbed the lock and chain as well as some bungee cords and quickly reattached it to the bumper near the broken hitch and fled the scene.

Next time at CB's, Bob was famously eighty-sixed before we even loaded in when he proceeded upon arrival to reach over the bar and grab a bottle of vodka. This was a trick that we had down to a science, but it required me to do something to distract the bar manager to give the other guy a chance to grab the bottle. The result of Bob's bottle attempt led to his being the earliest eighty-six in CBGB history. For the rest of the night we lobbied the staff to let Bob back into the venue, and I monitored him as he slept it off in the van. When the owner arrived and gave the okay just before show time, I couldn't get Bob to wake up. I went to the junkie deli and got a pack of NoDoz and a large coffee. I chilled it, added whiskey, and poured it down his throat in the van.

We pushed through the punters, who were patting Bob on the back as I cleared them away. The place was packed. Bob went into the dressing room and quickly downed a couple beers, then relieved himself into the empty cups. I watched him as he strode onto the stage to the fans' delight and placed the cups on the downstage deck, then turned to me and smiled as I handed him his guitar. A couple boys grabbed the cups and took big gulps before passing them around.

The show was a disaster, though I'm sure some found it highly entertaining. Far too early in the set I was singing Roger Miller and telling dirty jokes, and not long after that, Tommy stomped off the stage and left the club with his entourage in tow.

The next day when it was time to go to Boston, Tommy was nowhere to be found. As others searched, for our part, Paul and I went to the Blue and Gold and drank. It was nearly sunset when the van reappeared with Mars and Bob inside but still no Tommy. Carton was furious when he saw the condition I was in. So of course he told me to drive. I bought a twelve of Busch and grabbed the wheel. We careened up I-95 with the windows open, and Paul crushed pills into my beer. I guzzled as I drove, all the while fixing my makeup in the rearview mirror. Long lashes and smoky eyes, that's what would turn the tide.

We arrived at the Rat in Boston just as Tito and the Tarantulas had cleared the deck, and quickly threw up the backline. Tom, the Del Fuegos' bass player, filled in for Tommy and for a couple of songs it looked like it might work. But soon Paul grew bored and pulled me up to sing. At this point I was full cock, and in my mind I killed it that night. After the show a young disco singer with a panther tattooed on her head took me to a nearby flat. She handcuffed me to a red-hot radiator and put on Prince, disappeared into the kitchen, and returned with a bowl of ice.

The next morning I was due to meet the guys behind the venue so we could go back to Manhattan. Tommy had by now reappeared and was waiting for us in an East Village park. When I finally did get free and arrived sheepish and late, Carton wouldn't even look at me. I tried to explain that I was handcuffed to a radiator and couldn't get free, but he wasn't buying it. Paul took my hands and inspected my wrists and laughed and got in the van.

Butthole Surfers

One night we were playing a bill with the Butthole Surfers at City Gardens in Trenton, New Jersey. The Buttholes hadn't advanced the show, so they let us sound-check and they'd deal with it if and when the Buttholes arrived. Everyone was pretty cool at the City Gardens, but they ran a tight ship—they had to because the neighborhood was shit and the Gardens was mostly an all-ages venue so they had to be tough. But like most bands we had all sorts of ways to sneak bottles into clubs. I could get four pints in my cowboy boots alone.

The Buttholes did in fact show up and they were very scary. More scary than Flipper. The girl had a Manson-like scratch on her forehead so she could read it. Fuck. Then Paul came in out of breath. He had been on the pay phone outside in the street calling home and a mob of wilding youths were coming up the street toward him. He was like, "Everything's great, Mom, gotta run, bye." I wondered aloud if it was actually just the Buttholes showing up for the gig.

Off the Road but into the Studio

I was invited to the studio when the band was recording *Let It Be* at Blackberry Way studios in Dinkytown in Minneapolis. I made beer runs and Chinese food pickups and just kinda hung out and watched. Steve Fjelstad was mellow and cool, and it was just what I thought a recording session should be like. Carton was teching the sessions, and in that small little house the whole thing had a good vibe. You could tell this was going to be a cool record.

"Seen Your Video" had been played for a long time on tour at that point. I thought I remembered that it was once called "Sex with a Goat," and before that, the lyric was "I got steel that's cold." Seemed like Paul sabotaged that song. I first heard "Sixteen Blue" in a rehearsal in Boston during some time off. It was not long after Tommy had walked out on the band at CB's and gone missing, and he was sixteen years old then, so I just figured.

Peter asked me if he could have the picture I took of the inside of the van's sliding door. I couldn't find the negative because at the time I was using this weird disc camera that they stopped making film for and nobody could develop anymore. I had meant to make a band postcard to send to people from the road, saying something like, "This is what we see as we travel the country." You always had to keep a fine line with your significant

people: letting them know that you weren't having fun without them, but, also, that you weren't having *no* fun either.

With the recording of *Tim* I was the last man standing. No crew to speak of except myself, so I was studio tech. I got to work with Alex Chilton when he came in to do the demos, and it was a blast. He laid so much knowledge on everyone in such a short time. His production of "Left of the Dial" was superior to the one the label watered down for radio play.

But when the label took over, the producers came and the whole session became stiff. When the label had sucked all the air out of the studio, Paul called me in to sing, and we did all my hits: "Do the Clam," "If I Only Had a Brain," "Kansas City Star." The most difficult for me was the Soft Boys' classic "I Wanna Destroy You." I thought I had nailed that one for the first time ever, but when I went back into the control room I asked for a copy

and was told they had already recorded over it. I guess they figured I was too dumb to notice that the band hadn't even started another song yet. My guess was that even though Paul told them to record, they just never did.

I remember the *Tim* session best, though, when I picture Alex urging Bob into a great performance in an isolation booth.

One More for the Ditch

The now infamous *Saturday Night Live* appearance only happened because no one else would take the gig. That week's edition was preempted by a telethon hosted by Tony Danza—in most markets it was on at 3:00 a.m. Monday morning, if at all. When the band arrived they were noticeably agitated. Bob bounced past me on his tippy toes nervously chewing his nails, loudly asking everyone and no one which dressing room had belonged to Belushi. "I'm sure he left some drugs behind," Bob announced. Not much of an icebreaker.

Let It Be sessions

The managers and label execs were in abundance, so I spent most of the day messing with the rental gear. I always ordered extra in case they didn't like this amp or that cabinet. But tonight I decided to put the extra cabinets onstage. *SNL* suggested that I didn't realize this was television. I assured them I was aware.

The only cast members who spoke with me were Don Pardo and Don Novello, the comedian who played the chain-smoking Catholic priest Father Guido Sarducci, who was purported to be the rock critic for the *Vatican Enquirer*. Sam Kinison was also on the show. Novello told me that the show was trying to create a kind of late-night vibe shit with the lineup. Pardo laughed and cussed. It's true we were unwelcome by most everyone there, but I got the feeling that Kinison himself, along with the extras and even the bit players like Novello and Pardo, were not exactly feeling all that welcome by the stars.

At rehearsal we were too loud, and like every TV event I've done, the director complained that the cameramen couldn't hear the cuts. It went downhill from there. Everyone was trying hard to keep the band from drinking beer on set. So of course they broke out the vodka they had snuck in and soon not only the band was drinking but also the host. For the first song Bob came out wearing one of his mother-in-law's jumpsuits. Imagine her surprise sitting in the audience. The shocked looks on the faces of his wife and mother-in-law in the audience distracted him just enough from the lead line to make Paul turn and shout, "C'mon, fucker!" When I went to the green room between songs, I walked in on a very quiet scene. They were all looking at their shoes, and the pudding from the box lunches generously supplied by the show had been generously applied all over the walls.

Inquiring as to what had just occurred, Paul looked up and told me, "We got yelled at by the principal." Apparently, Lorne Michaels had just bawled him out for swearing on live TV. The label rep was angry because they'd gone out on a limb to get the Replacements on the show. The

SHOW #452   HOST: HARRY DEAN STANTON

                                   AIR: JANUARY 18, 1986

RUNDOWN FOR DRESS:

                                   RUNDOWN FOR RUNTHRU:

HERB COLD OPENING   1.   Opening Monologue
OPENING MONTAGE (VT)
OPENING MONOLOGUE   2.   Herb Cold Opening
STINK SALE   3.   Stink Sale
THAT BLACK GIRL (w/VT)
     Commercial #1   4.   Gunfighter

                                   5.   Hospital
GUNFIGHTER   6.   White Sale
DIE FOREIGNER DIE (VT)
WHITE SALE   7.   That Black Girl (w/VT)
     Commercial #2   8.   Cleveland Vice (w/VT)

                                   9.   Halfway House
HARRY INTRO
THE REPLACEMENTS #1 "Bastards of Young"   10. Big Ball of Sports (w/VT)
SAY NO (VT)
HOSPITAL   11. No Offense
     Commercial #3
     N.I./Station Break

UPDATE (w/VT)
     Commercial #4

CLEVELAND VICE (w/VT)
     Commercial #5

HARRY INTRO
SAM KINISON
     Commercial #6
     N.I./Station Break

HALFWAY HOUSE
     Commercial #7

HARRY INTRO
THE REPLACEMENTS #2 "Kiss Me On The Bus"
     Commercial #8
     BERKSHIRE PLACE PROMO

BIG BALL OF SPORTS (w/VT)
NO OFFENSE
     Commercial #9

GOODNIGHTS &
CREDITS

manager was upset because the band had snuck in a bottle of vodka. And I was upset that I wouldn't get any pudding.

I asked if we were still gonna play another song, and the silence was broken by Harry Dean Stanton, who was host that night, popping his head in the door saying, "One more for the ditch, fellas?" Cackling at full strength, Tommy pulled out the vodka, and soon Paul was telling Tommy to give him his clothes, to confuse Lorne Michaels. In no time everyone had swapped outfits for the second song except poor Bob, who would have to face his mother-in-law a second time.

Bombz Away

In July 1986, Gary Habib, the band's manager, called me and asked if I would roadie for the punk supergroup the Cherry Bombz. It seemed that their roadie had mysteriously disappeared in the middle of the night in Colorado, and they still had upcoming shows in Milwaukee, Indianapolis, Buffalo, Toronto, and New York.

I was would get $50 a show and a plane ticket home. It wasn't a good deal for me, but I loved New York City, and there was a girl there I wanted to see. On top of that, the band was made up of Johnny Thunders' pals Andy McCoy and Nasty Suicide of Hanoi Rocks, as well as Dave Tregunna, who was playing in Lords of the New Church with Stiv Bators—and was one of the twenty or so members of Sham 69. Their song "Borstal Breakout" was one that Jefferson's Cock covered (the football chant vocals being right up my atonal alley). The singer for the Bombz, Anita Chellemah, was from an all-girl pop band that was famous in England for their novelty hits. She was equally well known for falling off the stage and out of her clothes.

And my job? I was to tech for their drummer, Terry Chimes, aka Tory Crimes of The Clash. I looked over the drum setup with Mr. Chimes and made a diagram. Putting tape on the drum carpet to indicate where all the legs should live, I then marked the stands with my Sharpie so I could get the right height the next night. After sound check, he asked me to tell him more about "this organization" the Replacements that I belonged to: "What exactly is it?" he asked. "Some sort of affiliation of replacement roadies?" Mr. Chimes was the first vegan I would work with, but late at night when his wife was asleep, he would call my room and say, "Bill, can we go out for banana pancakes?"

Only one person showed up a few nights later when the Cherry Bombz played at the Vogue in Indianapolis. After that, Toronto was canceled, and the road manager tried to put me on a bus home. He was a giant bloke who had worked for the Damned and the Pistols, among others. But I stood up and told him, "You'll have to kill me to get the van keys from me." Furthermore, I was going to NYC and getting my $250 and plane ticket home. He only shook his head, and dropping his shoulders, he said, "This is the worst tour ever."

I parked the van at the Iroquois Hotel and went off to find a place to stay, since the girl I mentioned wasn't too thrilled to hear I was in town. So I called the only number I knew by heart, and Julie Pannabianco laughed her great laugh, saying, "Come on over." The next day when I went to the manager of the Bombz's office to get my money and ticket, he told me the band's van had disappeared overnight. Since he was paying me for five shows and I had only done three, he asked if I would be kind enough to find the van and get the backline to the Cat Club, where they had to play or risk returning the tour support and angering the media. I fetched the band's Finnish crew from the hotel and took him down to the impound lot where I had located their van. Racing back across Manhattan to beat the door time, we set up the gear. The show was saved for a full house of old punks and press and label execs.

And the Bombz broke up onstage in a drunken fistfight.

Lemon Gaol

It was the height of the Libyan conflict. The Americans had shot down two Libyan MIGs and Gaddafi had blown up a West German disco full of American servicemen. In retaliation, Reagan had bombed Gaddafi's house, killing his kid. And the terrorists promised more violence against Americans. At the same time, Chernobyl had melted down causing radioactive gas to float over Europe as far as Italy, causing boycotts on milk. Every American band from Green on Red to Neil Young had canceled their tours in Europe, but not the Replacements. Although mostly ambivalent about the whole "opportunity" to tour Europe, the Replacements also realized that, not unlike *Saturday Night Live,* if they canceled, there was a good chance they would never be invited back. Besides, we didn't drink milk.

Before we left I had a local artist from my neighborhood paint my cowboy boots like an American flag and a red, white, and blue bull's-eye on the back of my thrift store carport jacket—which I wore proudly around Europe until we reached Milan, where it looked as if the Libyan migrants would take me up on my offer. I still wore the boots (I had no other manly footwear with me) but turned the jacket inside out, exposing an orange lining like a deer hunter hoping not to get shot.

I was already immediately let down at discovering our arrival was at Gatwick rather than Heathrow. After clearing customs, we were picked up by our English tour manager (T.M.) in a "splitter van," sort of an English version of a Japanese garbage truck. The ample free drinks in the smoking section of coach had done nothing to reduce my already ample jet lag. Bob quickly nicknamed the T.M. "Cloud," and we began to insult everyone by our mere presence.

Arriving in London in June 1986, we checked out the Averard Hotel, a famous rock hotel: like the Iroquois and the Tropicana, it was also dingy and infested. Our room had two single cots jammed next to each other, and the hall door or the bathroom door could not be opened if the other was ajar. Realizing we would be stacked up like inmates in a cell, we went out to the stoop and loitered, against all wishes of our local innkeepers, and waited for the pub across the street to open. The liquor laws in London being very strict, we had to wait until 11 a.m. for the pub at the corner to open. When it did, I was first in line with a fresh pocket of British pounds courtesy of our British tour manager, which we quickly spent on warm pints and short whiskies. Since we didn't need to tip, we lost the change from our per diems in the gambling machines. Somehow, I was still able to drink my fill and even get a cucumber sandwich into my belly before going back to the room and passing out.

Our first show in London was at the legendary Dingwall's in Camden, a basement club for punks and rockers that resided under a more popular disco. We were told Robyn Hitchcock and Lemmy Kilmister would be in the house, but for me the real treat was meeting a bloke claiming to have been Johnny Thunders' London roadie. Bob's rented Marshall amp kept blowing fuses at sound check, and he showed me that replacing the fuse with the foil from a pack of Dunhills would not only solve the fuse issue by completing the current but would allow the amp to run hotter and louder. I asked him if that wouldn't blow the whole amp without the fuse as a fail-safe, to which he replied, "Oh, most certainly."

The promoter had left half a dozen pitchers of ales and bitters back-stage, all of them too warm and strong for the band's liking. I noticed a case of Schlitz cans on the floor behind the stage and was able to barter for a case and what appeared to be the scarcest commodity in England, a bit of ice. Taking the pitchers of bitters out to the audience, I passed them to the kids in the audience as they were clearly not drunk enough.

Before we went on, I was honored to bring Lemmy from Motörhead to the dressing room and introduce him to Paul, who taking his hand asked, "Can you Lemmy a couple quid?"

They opened the show with the Marines' hymn and blasted through the set. It was too loud for Lemmy. When Bob's rented Marshall blew up (as anticipated), it allowed me to close the show with a little "Kansas City Star."

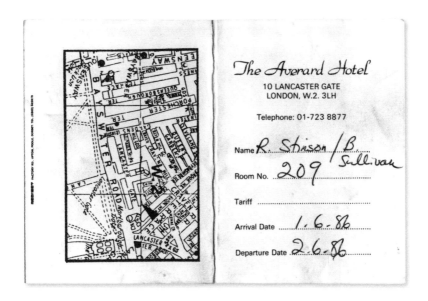

The Averard Hotel

10 LANCASTER GATE
LONDON, W.2. 3LH

Telephone: 01-723 8877

Name *R. Stinson / B. Sullivan*

Room No. *209*

Tariff

Arrival Date *1.6.86*

Departure Date *2.6.86*

We had to get up and hit the French consulate early the next morning to get our visas. Due to the uncomfortable state of our rooms, I left Bob to sleep and retired to the bar where I was joined by our sound guy, Monty Lee Wilkes. We only intended to drink until they asked us to leave, but they never did ask us to leave, and soon enough they set up breakfast around us and we were hammered. Some recall that we then caused a scene at the French consulate, but as I remember it, I was merely holding up Monty or he was holding me up. We still got our papers and gave the band a taste of their own medicine. Something no one likes.

The next day we jumped into the Splitter and ferried across the channel to the Continent and stopped in Belgium for the night. We wandered the center of town trying to find a bar, only to finally choose a loud and crowded disco full of coked-up Euro trash. Leaving Paul behind, Bob and I wandered out to the market where we commandeered a guitar from some buskers and played a little "Kansas City Star" for the tourists, then got chased away when Bob attempted to take all the tips from the case on the ground.

Returning to the disco where we had left Paul, we found it was now on fire and people were running out as the sirens screamed and the fire trucks blocked our vantage. I asked around if anyone had seen an American with Westerbergian hair and one orange shoe but to no avail. Then I spotted Paul on a pay phone across the street. He was pleading with his girl at home and was oblivious to the uproar—he had the handset firm to one ear and a finger in the other. I never left him behind again, remembering Mel Brooks's words: "Gentlemen, we must protect our Phony Baloney Jobs."

I inquired from Cloud how far it was to "Amp-sterdam" so I could replace Bob's amp. Cloud wasn't too happy to find this out after we had already left London, but I did it because I'd heard from Lemmy that Audio Amsterdam had far superior rentals than what we had gotten in London. We were always up against the "pros" who thought they knew what we needed better than I did, since I was such a rookie, but they always discovered eventually what I learned early: if the band didn't like it, they broke it.

While in Holland I bought a variety of hash and weed, and after eating a famous space cake I walked the circular city, lost for several hours, meeting a young woman at a face painting booth and got my face painted in order to make her acquaintance. I purchased a bugle from the Dutch cavalry with most of my funds, and when I couldn't find the hotel ("It's on the canal," I kept saying), I got in a cab and told the driver how many guilders I had left and asked if he could take home for about that. He grunted at me, then drove around the corner, threw it in park, and said, "You are here."

Still tripping during the show that night, I was sure I saw a handgun in the crowd and ran out to protect Paul, only to realize it was a hallucination. The band stopped and looked at me. I shrugged and slunk offstage. When the show was over, the girl I'd met face painting was gone.

On our way to the border, I had saved one joint for the ride and told Cloud to let me know when I needed to get rid of it. In a misunderstanding, he told me to get rid of it—but I thought I had time to smoke it. When I lit up, everyone (except Bob) was freaking out, yelling at me to throw it out the window, as we were just then arriving at the border. Even Tommy lit up a cigarette in an attempt to mask the smell. We made it through the border. Stopping for gas, I went around to fill up the tank and there was my half-smoked joint, stuck to the rain on the side of the van.

In Paris, Bob loved that the toilets were just holes in the floor. On later tours my pal Brendan Macabre called them Munsons, after his favorite Yankee catcher, Thurman Munson. Bob just loved that he didn't have to aim.

I wondered what we were promoting there in Paris, because it seemed that the locals couldn't afford albums and stereos, so I guess it was just American Goodwill. Bob was upset with the cost of a couple eggs at the bistro, and he told me he could get a couple dozen for that price. And besides, he added, if it wasn't for America, they would be eating German eggs. At the Rex Club in Paris the band had acquired some duty-free vodka and tore through a set to the silent crowd that seemed disturbed at times and rapt at others. Bob and Paul began to arm-wrestle over the bottle and ended up on the floor in an all-out tussle, at which point Bob broke the now-empty bottle on the riser and put it to Paul's throat. The stunned silence in the room was loud and Cloud whispered in my ear, "What do we do now?"

"Wait," I said. They seldom went much further—and right on cue Bob laughed and tossed the jagged glass aside, joining Chris and Tommy, who had never stopped playing while the entire room stood gape-mouthed.

Paul was opening every night then with the Marines' hymn, replacing the lyrics with "We will fight *your* country's battles," and most nights ended in chaos. Which was good for me, because then I got to sing. Also every night, Paul and Tommy would astound the crowd by dumping beer on the stage for the proper "traction." The locals were astounded by the "American Waste." I wondered if when they whistled at us that meant that they liked us or didn't. Either way, they were whistling a lot.

When we got to Germany, we discovered we had to pay to use the toilets, so we didn't. In Italy, Cloud took a wrong turn and we ended up trapped in a neighborhood nestled on the top of a hill. As we tried to back the Splitter back down, we caused a terrible snarl in traffic and the locals whistled and threw trash out their windows at us, which further confused me about the meaning of whistling overseas.

In Perugia we played a nightclub owned by mobsters to a packed house of stunned students, unclear how a band would come such a great distance to suck. When it was over and the disco music kicked in, they crowded the floor and quickly forgot us in the fog and (I assume) in their heads. The next day I was tired of riding in the Splitter and hitched a ride with our Italian promoter in his sports car. He roared up the mountains at well over 100 mph with Sanford and Son–like trucks laden down with produce and such blocking the lanes. When he was using the "shoulder" to pass, I could see

Into the Lemon Jail

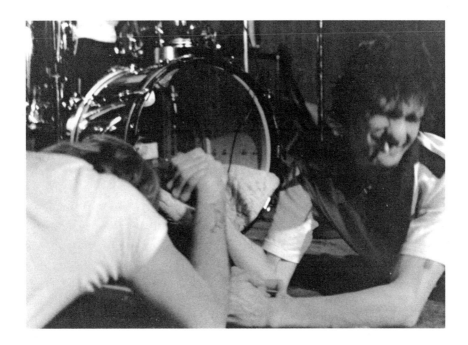

down into the ravines as gravel flew, and he laughed at my distress. At the apex of the peaks he stopped at a wayside where we drank espressos and dined on dainty cakes before he roared down to Milan, beating the band by hours. I sat in a charming café watching old men play a tabletop version of bocce and drank coffee and licorice liquor, the toothless old chaps smiling and nodding at me, allowing me the first day of the trip where I totally got what Europe was supposed be like. Then the band arrived.

That night a group of skinheads came and skated around for the opener, keeping the floor clear of the frightened exchange students and curious locals. The promoter asked me how I would deal with the menacing group of skankers. *How would I deal with it?* I thought to myself, telling the promoter that somehow Paul always knew how to handle a crowd with his guitar and that the skins would tire of the whole event before long when they didn't have the familiar chunk of local punks to fuel them.

As I set up for the show Cloud approached me. "Bill," he said quietly, "Bob's done heroin. What should we do?" *Now it's we,* I thought to myself. I told him not to worry: what it is, it is; what will be, will be. And the band tore it up for the mostly American crowd. And the skinheads? Well, they had supplied the drugs to Bob and were now nodding in the corners themselves, no longer a menace. Monty, for his part, had met a beautiful young Italian girl who after the show asked me in her cute broken English what we were doing after. I mimed to her that I was going to the hotel to sleep, to which she exclaimed, "Zleep? Monty no zleep!"

That night in the hotel Bob turned blue in his bed and stopped breathing. I banged on his massive chest and shook him, to no response. Looking at the antique phone . . . 911? Hell. I dragged him to the shower, which as luck would have it had no curtain or door or tub, and put him under a cold spray (like there was even hot water) and slapped him on the face, dreading mouth to mouth. He sputtered awake, and when he saw I had him down on the cold tile in his underwear, he roared and tossed me over the bidet (the *second toilet,* as Bob liked to call it), uprooting it from the floor.

"I thought you were dead!" I shouted, and he stopped hitting me.

"Really?" he replied, then toweled off and went to bed with a sandwich he had hidden in the duvet.

At that moment the phone rang out in that Euro sputtering ring, and it was the front desk. Thinking the noise had caused a complaint I shouted into the receiver that everything was fine. The voice on the other end told me that the brothers of Monty's new friend were in the lobby inquiring about her location. I gave him Monty's room number and went to bed.

When we arrived in Spain, I was able to access some absinthe and hash and was in a chill mood. We invited the Chambermaids, who were all sisters, to the show and they arrived all dolled up and ready to go. After the show their brothers showed up ready to go as well.

On the drive back north the windshield wiper (yes, singular) broke in

Into the Lemon Jail

a raging rainstorm. Monty fixed his belt to the wiper and when Cloud said pull, Monty stood in the trough of the passenger door and pulled to clear the screen. That and the fact that we were now late, *and* driving on the other side of the road with a right-hand drive and in the mountains, made for a tense drive, but I had hash to eat while washing it down with absinthe.

Back in the UK we appeared on the famous TV show *The Old Grey Whistle Test*. More whistling, I thought to myself, very confused. It's interesting that when they released the anniversary video of performers who appeared on the show, the Replacements were left off. Arriving at Gatwick for our return trip, the old bloke at security looked at Paul and said, "I saw you on the telly last night."

"What did you think?" asked Paul.

"Step into this little room, please" was the reply.

Back in the USA

On our return to the USA, we had a short East Coast run that cut across the southeast finishing up in New Orleans. When we arrived at Logan Airport in Boston, I was waiting around for the guitars as everyone got their own bags. I guess crossing international borders as tour manager was something management figured I could now handle. I was approached by a young woman in the baggage area who asked me if we were a band, and I admitted that we were the Replacements from Minneapolis and just returning from a European tour. She told me she went to college in Boston and had seen us on different occasions, and that she was a translator for immigration and customs.

I told her we were very tired, turned on the ol' charm, and convinced her to help me circumnavigate the long line with all my guitars. She went and got me a skycap (a sort of airport porter) to load up my cases on a cart and had an immigration officer come over and stamp our passports. I asked her if she wanted to come down to a show and she politely declined.

Chris, having had enough of everyone's shenanigans at borders, snuck off by himself, got in line, and ignored me when I tried to motion him over. The skycap then led us to customs and expedited our gear through. I handed him a couple twenties and he said, "Why don't you fellows head to your gate and take a load off?" and said he would get our gear onto our connecting flight.

When we got to Long Island, a local radio DJ came backstage with a bottle of Jack Daniels (now we had two) and challenged the band to a drinking contest. Paul had been told that this DJ was an important figure, so rather than insulting him as usual he drank him under the table. The result, however, was that now Paul was also pretty drunk. His voice was burning out, and rather than not having a voice in NYC the next day, he eventually called me onstage and I took over with "Kansas City Star," "The Clam," "Eighteen," and all my hits before the band tore it up to finish the set. They weren't the only ones to tear things up that night: the crowd destroyed the main floor of the club, even pushing the sound booth back about ten feet.

As I was picking up cables and packing guitars and the lights came up, I heard the club's bouncer thanking everyone over the PA and urging them to clear out of the now-closed venue, as well as reminding them to come down the next night for the Ramones.

At the Ritz the first of two nights was sold out; in fact, it was oversold to the point where the street was full of people trying to get in. It seemed that we had gone over the top and had become the it place to be. It got so out of control that the NYPD had to put up wooden horses on the end of Eleventh Street and bring the mounted division to try and control the unruly crowd. Inside the band was quiet and relatively sober. The crowd was not. They were piqued and drinking hard, and when the video screen went up and the band tore into "Bastards of Young," Tommy did a standing long jump of nearly twenty feet from his amp to the monitor line, while at the same time the crowd surged against the stage causing it to shake like the earth was moving, almost knocking over the backup guitars in their stands. What followed was the best show the band ever played.

The next night was different. With all day to sit around the Gramercy Hotel, Paul had time to get nervous and drink. At sound check most of our rider beer was already gone and the Jack was at halfmast. Chris and I went out for food but instead hit a number of bars and came back kind of knackered ourselves, and when the show was not sold out, the New Management Team, along with the promoters, tried to hold back the show time between Steve Earle and the 'Mats.

Out of booze, Paul had to get sneaky. Years later, opening for Bright Eyes at Town Hall, both Steve and his brother told me the exact same story of Paul coming into their dressing room and making small talk while he reached his hand behind his back, fishing through the cold melted ice for bottled treasure.

The band became unruly and the crowd was even worse. Many in the audience had attended both shows and had clearly been drinking for two days straight, and when Bob got up onstage behind the video screen and began playing along with Joe Perry on the guitar line of the "Walk This Way" video (featuring Run DMC), they began to throw drinks at the million-dollar video system, pelting the screen and stage and sound system. I mentioned to the Higher Ups that this could only turn out bad if they didn't raise the screen, but as usual I was disregarded by the professionals. Soon the whole band was playing along to Aerosmith and the crowd was getting wild. Security got nervous and began to fortify their positions. Normally, I could tell security what to do, as I had the night before,

and handle the crowd by myself. Tonight, there was no way I was going to handle what was about to happen when they finally raised the screen. It was like rats fleeing the ocean only to get on a sinking ship. Security tossed them back into the water as fast as they flooded the deck. Paul went into "Eighteen," and there was no way I was going to reprise my performance—besides, I had my hands full with kids who were getting past security and grabbing at the spare guitars and Tommy's cocktails. I gave one an airplane spin and tossed him over the top rope. Fines and suspensions were no doubt in line after this match. Tommy danced one stage crasher up to the monitor line where I kneeled down behind him so Tommy could give the kid a schoolyard push over me and off the stage.

Looking toward center stage I saw Paul pull John deVries of Agitpop up to sing the Alice Cooper standard only to have security grab him by his elbows and carry him from the stage. I ran over and obtained his release

Into the Lemon Jail

and handed him the mic to finish the song. Then Paul dove into the crowd, first walking on them like Jesus on the choppy seas, then as he began to sink into the surf a security guard grabbed him by the hand and pulled him back aboard.

The next morning I was packed and ready to go when Cloud came into the bar where I was ogling Paul Shaffer and said, "I guess you better start heading to Minneapolis." I thought to myself, "Is this how I'm to be fired? I'm the pigeon for last night's meltdown?" But then Cloud told me Paul's hand was broken and the tour was canceled.

Not long after that show Bob was fired, and soon after I found myself sitting in a booth at the Uptown Bar where I had been called for a band meeting. Good, I thought, assuming this might be the end of my run. At least they have the balls to fire me to my face. But instead I sat in the corner of a vinyl retro booth as the band fired their longtime manager and the man who had discovered them, Peter Jespersen. The look on his face was that of a blindsided lover. He looked me in the eye, and I had nothing. I was as shocked as he was. But even more shocked to find out I still had a job.

LOVE IT TO DEATH

In April 1987, *Pleased to Meet Me* was done but not yet released, and the band had a new guitarist. Slim Dunlap had taken over for Bob Stinson. A great choice for sure. Slim had been my personal cheerleader for years, and I knew that he would be easygoing on and off the stage, even though his pedal setup was a homemade Frankenstein of rebuilt parts and bodies. He insisted on setting up his own guitars and pedals, and all I had to do was make sure his amps were hot.

At the start of tour Monty and I drove down in the first nice van we ever had. I had been promoted to tour manager for a short run in Florida, and the plan was to rent a minivan for me to drive the band around in while Monty and the tech would handle the beautiful new van. I had rented this beautiful new van in Minneapolis by lying through my teeth to the neighborhood party rental guy that we would be "up north" fishing for a couple weeks. As long as nothing went wrong, he would never be the wiser. Plus Slim knew how to reset the mileage.

I mean, really, what could go wrong on a Replacements tour?

We started out in April, just like on my first tour, in Jacksonville at a great little coffee shop called Einstein a Go-Go, a tiny venue run by two sisters who had hosted great shows in their day. With the new album not being out yet, I think the idea was to get the kinks out with the new guitar slinger. And perhaps with the new tour manager as well? The first few shows went off without much of a hitch. In Melbourne, we saw the Twins training facility. In Cocoa Beach, our hotel pool was shaped like a space shuttle. When we got to the Cameo on Collins Avenue in Miami Beach, the Art Deco revival was just under way and our hotel was all pastels and thin walls.

While I was waiting at the bar for the band to come down, the happy hour entertainment was Dr. John. He walked behind the booze on an elevated stage behind the bar, sat down at a spinet, pulling an alarm clock and some sheet music out of his briefcase. Placing the sheet music above the keys and the clock on the top of the spinet, he wound the clock and started playing without saying a word. I know I waited forty-five minutes exactly for the band because when the alarm went off, the good Dr. put the clock and the music back in the case and walked away.

By the time we got to Tallahassee we had been partying pretty hard ever since Miami. The venue in Tallahassee gave us the kitchen for a dressing room, and for the rest of my career, I never let that happen again. That

night the band put flour from the pantry in their hair and towels from the closet in their pants and shirts and asked to be intro'd as the Retirements.

After the show I took Tommy's beer away from him, explaining that he was underage and drinking in a police parking lot. But I could tell I had embarrassed him in front of his fans. Just then I heard a crash and turned around to see that Monty had wrapped the bumper of the beautiful new rental van around a pole.

Every year since, the club booker from Tallahassee and I see each other in Atlanta, where he is now a successful promoter, and we laugh about how we both got fired that night.

Paul got married in Southfield, Michigan, north of Detroit, later that year. Having no money I rode the Amtrak to downtown Detroit and from there tried to catch a bus but missed it, so I had to cab it up to the wedding. The wedding band was our good friends and perennial openers the Young Fresh Fellows, and our other support act and labelmates, Agitpop, were in the house as well, so the reception was a little raucous. I embarrassed myself by trying to dance with Paul rather than his bride.

Later, or maybe earlier, all of us roadies were in the restroom smoking weed when the Replacements' manager came in and stepped up to a urinal. He was wearing an expensive (I assume) silk suit, and he was making small talk with me as I sat on the sink smoking, when the Agitpop roadie turned and shook before zipping up, sending pee spots all up and down the leg of the manager's silk suit.

The next morning I was trying to get a cab back to Detroit but found that Southfield cabbies refused service to the city. The hotel valet pointed out to me that there were three school buses full of Blue Jay fans going to Tiger Stadium. He suggested that they wouldn't notice one more person, so I threw my tuxedo over my shoulder and slipped onto the last bus. It was overcrowded, so I squatted in the aisle near the exit, looking conspicuously inconspicuous. I seemed to be getting away with it when, as we neared the center of the city, one of the three buses broke down and forced the consolidation of riders onto the two remaining buses.

Rather than stay and try to explain myself, I figured I was close enough now to get a cab. I got off the bus on the side of the highway and walked up the embankment. I climbed over a fence, and as I began to walk down the frontage road a spotless Cadillac pulled up next to me and slow-rolled beside me, sort of sizing me up. The neighborhood looked a little rough and I was beginning to get nervous when the electric window came down and an older gentleman motioned me over. He told me to get in. As we drove silently down the road his wife looked back at me and smiled meekly. But the driver said nothing until he dropped me off at a hospital, since, as he now told me, that was where I was bound to end up walking around that neighborhood with a tuxedo over my shoulder.

I arrived at the Detroit Amtrak station too late to catch the train, so I walked over to Tiger Stadium after all and found it was only $2.50 to sit in the left field bleachers for what would be the deciding game of the 1987 Eastern Division, and the winner would then travel to Minneapolis to face the Twins in the Metrodome. I sat out in the bleachers with the locals and cheered hard for the Tigers. I was taken in like Oliver Twist and was soon sharing pin joints of weed and flasks of cognac and had made fast friends with the Tiger fans, until one of them asked me why I was cheering so hard for the Tigers if I was a Twins fan.

I replied that the Blue Jays had always had our number but I thought we had a chance against the aging Tigers. They all got real quiet at first, but then the ball trickled through Toronto's all-star shortstop's legs. The Tigers had won the East, sending them to Minnesota, and we were all friends again.

Last Stops on the Road

On our tour with Petty in 1989, the first few shows weren't sold out, and once again we couldn't help feeling that not everyone was happy we were there. The band really hadn't started to act out, and the early set time may have had something to do with that. It wasn't really the Heartbreakers who were throwing the chill, and guys like Mike Campbell and Belmont Tench reached out to Paul and Tommy, and the Scottish monitor engineer took a shine to me when we bonded over the fact that I fell asleep in a red ants' nest in Texas after a show and he slept in the reeds at Jones Beach a couple weeks later and came back covered in chigger bites.

Petty himself even sat with me one afternoon and we had a very nice conversation about music and politics. He introduced me to his family and was maybe not warm but very friendly; I'm guessing he wasn't sure if I was in the band or not. I asked his daughter if she liked living in Los Angeles and of course she did. Then she asked me if I knew who Charo was. "Of course," I said. "Do you live in Charo's old house? I've seen it on the map to the star homes," I said. But she stopped me and said that no, they lived in the home of the doctor who did Charo's breasts.

When it came down to it, it was more the big-time promoters who saw little to no future in the Replacements and who treated us as the great unwashed. To be fair, we did seldom wash, but they foolishly thought by holding out on the beer and whiskey we could be contained. Clearly, they had never heard of per diem or liquor stores and tour bus coolers. And not having something for Paul to throw against the wall when he walked in the room or for Tommy to pour into his hair for his morning "rooster bath" did nothing to stop us from drinking. Also, the crew's reluctance to share their weed was not only contrary to stoner etiquette of the time but was also fruitless: I had just as good connections for green and white as they had; I just didn't have the big pharma connections that the big stars had. Yet. In fact, the only time I remember Petty's crew offering me some weed was when we had to cross the border from Toronto overnight and they needed to get rid of it. The Toronto border, I thought to myself. No thanks.

Before shows on the Petty tour, we'd regularly be sitting in a completely empty cinder-block bunker of a dressing room. Hell, they didn't even give us chairs. One night in Tennessee the band was dangling their legs off the makeup counter and I was unscrewing the majority of the bright light bulbs that lined the mirrors to create "ambulance," as Paul called it, when Petty walked in and asked, "Is this how you're treated every night?" Kind of a high point, we said. He turned on his heels and you could hear him scream at the top of his lungs. (In my mind, he was telling the promoter that we don't have to live like refugees.) In mere minutes, a chain of white-coated caterers came in with wheeled carts stacked with snacks and drinks and even booze, while hands brought in sofas and chairs.

I followed Petty through the venue as he dressed down the promoter and his own reps like an executive in a '40s movie. They were all trying to keep up with him as he went out to a VIP area between the seats and the lawn where fine dining tables were being set up for the big spenders. He shouted that he had not okayed this bullshit, and that the people on the lawn were more important to him than the bankers and lawyers, and something about how MCI Center must stand for the promoter's "friends and family" and not his fans. When the workers continued about their job of setting down the crystal and china, he lost it and began turning over tables and smashing plates until he had their attention. A little while later he reappeared at our door and asked if everything was okay. We meekly said yes.

To repay his kindness the Replacements of course snuck into his dressing room and stole his wife's clothes and hit the stage in drag, trashing the backline and tossing Chris's drums into the crowd. It was not unusual for Tommy or Paul to toss a drum or two, and usually I was able to retrieve them, but not always. One time I chased a floor tom in vain around the crowded midway of a fair that a kid carried over his head like a snake basket. Mars's kit was multicolored and assembled from different brands—whatever I could find in the next town worked for him. Only the snare was not easily replaced. Usually, I was able to grab it before Tommy, but one night while he had my attention Paul grabbed it and ran to chuck it into the crowd. I gunned off the arena deck and caught it in midair, landing in the pit among the security guards, who then tried to throw me out. That night,

Repaying Tom Petty's kindness

after throwing Mars's drums into the crowd, the band then proceeded to break the new furniture in the dressing room and smash Heineken bottles on the walls.

By the time the tour wound down, however, everyone was getting along fine. We all even went to a bar in Colorado one night and took over the stage as the boy band version of Jefferson's Cock, with Paul and Petty on guitar, Tommy on bass, and Tench on keys and I put out my best version of "Indian Reservation" behind the chain-link fence that surrounded the stage. It was amazing and had to be the best Jefferson's Cock ever, which is better than you might think. Jeffersons's Cock, or The Cock as it came to be known, was an evolving and moveable feast that began one night in Lawrence, Kansas, in 1983. Lawrence was an early stronghold for the band because of college radio and the connection between Lawrence bands like the Micronotz.

In 1983, Lawrence was the first show of the tour, with the next one being all the way east in Nashville a couple days later. Peter rented a single hotel room in a strip motel, and we were all going to sneak in the back, but the problem was we got caught and evicted. Our DJ pals from KCRW bailed us out, and they decided to have us play at their house while we were there, because why not?

Paul decided we were going to play the party as Jefferson's Cock, a name he just pulled out of his ass. Tommy and Bob were not involved, but Carton played bass and Mars played drums. We got into the roommates' closets (do you see a pattern forming here?) and dressed in housedresses and combat boots, which was the look at the time by the women who hung out at the Hüsker shows. We spent the afternoon painting our eyes and powdering our noses and then did a set of covers including "You Think I'm Psycho (Don't You, Mama)," "Mrs. Brown, You've Got a Lovely Daughter," "Borstal Breakout," and of course, "Eighteen," "Kansas City Star," and "Do the Clam."

After our "set," a farm girl took me in her pickup out in the fields, and when I got back, everyone (meaning Carton) was mad because we were supposed to leave. So I had to drive much of the way as penance. When we got out of the van in Nashville, parked on Elliston Place, Paul and I were sitting on the curb with a little mascara running down our faces, waiting for the liquor store to open when he said to me, "I think I know what the shakes feel like." Tommy came up and said he was going to go find some Nu Nile hair slick, because he was sick of Murray's.

The next time The Cock arose it was in Boston on a night off. Mitch, the manager of the Rat, had been replaced by Jane and Julie, who were much

more open to the new wave of rock and roll, and they encouraged us to re-create Jefferson's Cock for new band night.

We had more than ample help for this show and showed up in severe makeup (Paul had gotten a diagram and instructions from a beautician he had met in Ohio). We also had housedresses and boots. We hit the stage with no sound check and little gear of our own and gave them the Hits, this time adding a little Gary Glitter. After our set a little sweaty guy in an ill-fitting three piece came back and told us he wanted to sign us to his label. Pulling out an enormous ziplock full of blow, he shouted, *How much of this will it take to make the deal?* and dumped it on the carved-up cable-wheel table full of beer ashes and tahini. As we were digging the last crystals out of the grooves, security arrived and made him leave.

The demise of The Cock was the same old story: too hard, too fast. We played a show at the Entry that came together when we were set to open for the Suburbs and the Suicide Commandos' cover band Giant Shrimp. It was an event. A local dressmaker made me a housedress only Liza Minnelli would wear, and I did a naked photo shoot in a bathtub for a calendar when Paul decided we were going to wear overalls and straw hats and do a surprise skiffle set with boxes and strings. And it went as badly as it possibly could, possibly because we could only find a handful of unmarked pills to split.

To be honest, I tried to milk The Cock for rent money, hiring a horn section even, to try and make up for Paul and Tommy's departures, but we just never really got it up. So The Cock only came out three times. But, really, anytime I was lucky enough to front the Replacements onstage or in the studio, I felt like a Cock.

Different Kinds of Cake

On my last tour with the Replacements, one of my last shows was when we flew in from the Midwest to perform on a new awards show in New York City. The International Music Awards were held in the Armory at Twenty-fifth and Lexington, home of the Fighting 69th—the famed Irish regiment immortalized in the Jimmy Cagney movie. The star power was crazy: Keith, Ozzy, Tina, Alice, Robert Palmer. To say the least, we were not the focus of the day's attention. Loading-in early in the morning we then sat around for eight hours. Around lunchtime, thoroughly bored, I took to the street and found an Irish pub, where I proceeded to get into a drunken argument with the locals about Christy Moore and Luka Bloom. I left them with an "Up the Rebels" and returned to the stage where we were still behind schedule. Tommy grabbed me and dragged me down to Alice Cooper's dressing room to meet him. Barging in without knocking, Tommy slingshot me in front of his body and announced, "Alice Cooper! Meet your biggest fan." Alice and someone from his staff stood in the middle of the room wrestling with a pair of skintight leather pants, trying to pull them up over the Coop's bikini briefs.

After sound check we needed a nap and found an out-of-the-way room not being used by the production and passed out on a couch. I was woken up by voices: "There's someone in the corner," one voice said. "Just a roadie," said another. A group was sitting around the table, and at first I thought they were eating dinner in the dark. I was happy I hadn't missed that. Upon focusing, I recognized members of several prominent bands huddled around a towering pile of coke, scooping gold and black credit cards into it like it was onion dip. "Should we offer him some?" said the first voice. "Nah," said the group. I nodded as I left, a gesture aimed at no one in particular, just in their general direction in case one of them bothered to look.

It was, in fact, dinnertime, so I waddled out to catering—part sleepy, part drunk, part disappointed—and got in line behind Ric Ocasek and Paulina Porizkova. Tommy joined me and said, way too loudly, "How did *he* get a woman like that?" Barely turning in acknowledgment, the Cars' guitarist gave himself a casual karate chop halfway down his thigh with an even slighter smile.

After I had my main course I perused the dessert table, and after making my choice of cake I turned too abruptly and bumped into Ozzy. Now I was never the hugest Sabbath fan: they were a band that I had little experience with in my youth and had only became fully acquainted with them on 'Mats tours. But here in the presence of the Prince of Darkness, I suddenly got it. Bowing down, my dessert fell on the floor, to which Ozzy mumbled, "You've dropped your cake."

Returning to the only place a roadie can feel comfortable, I went back to the stage.

"Talent Show" was the song that had been chosen, as the label wanted to release it as a single (or had released it as a single—it was usually hard to tell the difference with most of my bands). I found out from the band that the network censors were concerned about the line in the song about "feeling good from the pills we took" and wanted the band to change the lyric. I believe they had arrogantly even come up with acceptable substitutions. Paul didn't really refuse to change the song; he simply refused to acknowledge the creeps at all, and they took that as an insult.

We had the great Yik Wong onstage to handle all circumstances, and it was only one song with little chance of stage divers, so I went out to the TV truck and spoke with the sound engineer about cues. The censors approached me and inquired if the band was changing the lyric. I told them that was above my pay grade, and as the band began playing they became more and more irate with me, demanding that I let them know or they would have to "push the button," because there was no delay.

I stood silent as Paul approached the offending line, and when the time came, the censor with the icy trigger finger hit the dump button and censored the lyric while Paul simultaneously censored himself. As the network lackeys sat back, content with a job well done, Paul could be heard changing the lyric "It's too late to turn back" to "It's too late to take pills" over and over again. Here we go.

The End

Toward the end, when I wasn't riding in the semi with the driver known simply as the Wizard, I rode from town to town in the back of a bus, sleeping on a lumpy couch no cleaner than the poop-covered furniture of the past. Many people don't know this, but the Replacements played to big crowds in their day. By the late '80s they had graduated to bigger shows, often at the same colleges where just years earlier we had played house parties and

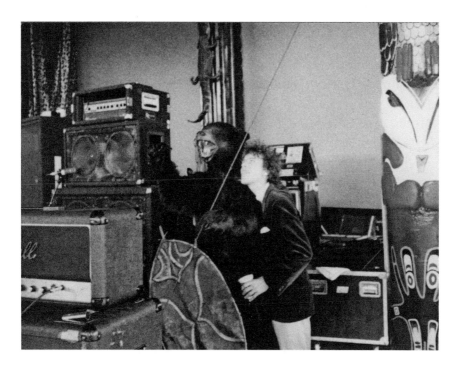

Rathskellers. But in the hockey rinks and amphitheaters around the country, it seemed my friends were no longer welcome as the opening band or to hang around backstage.

I was becoming a reasonably good stage manager, all the time watching my old friends succumbing to the brownnosing of toadies. Around this time Paul and Tommy said *poop* all the time. In Europe they said *les poop*. It's true that Paul was called the louse. But he didn't really step in poop before he went inside NYC buildings. There was poop everywhere, and it was hard to avoid. So, really, who didn't walk into buildings in New York in the '80s with some poop on their shoe?

After Paul and Tommy came back from recording *Pleased to Meet Me,* I saw that things had changed. Management told me I couldn't hire local sound companies or crew. The guys I was now paired with on the bus were all good dudes, but it just wasn't my scene anymore. The Memphis-ication of the 'Mats had transformed them into rock stars. "Garfield Babylon"— what I'd jokingly called our stretch of Minneapolis between the CC Club and the Lake Harriet Rose Garden—had been replaced with "Beale Street Babylon," and sidekicks like me had been replaced with personal assistants and underlings. Scoring a few lines and pints just didn't compare to what the pros could purloin.

I concentrated on Mars and the new guitarist, Slim, who oddly enough was that same janitor at a Minneapolis nightclub who had given me the courage to succeed in the first place and gallons of advice on cars and guitars and how to live your life. Bob Dunlap was a good cat to learn from. He had this thing where at the end of his show, he would get the broom and sweep up. I guess that's really what I was doing every night, too. Learning how to swamp a stage.

But more and more, I was understanding that although my days on the road with the Replacements had been a life-changing experience, I could sense it was grinding to a halt. A sporadic touring schedule and the loss of brotherhood were taking a toll on us all. At the same time, I was able to

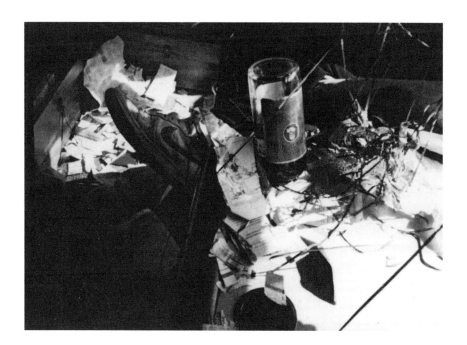

travel extensively with Soul Asylum. Dave Pirner was from my 'hood, Dan Murphy had the kind of drive that seemed to be missing in the Replacements' camp, and Karl Mueller was the kind of friend anyone would want in their life.

The Replacements, though, would always be the definition of my career in music, and while we helped change the music world by not adhering to the common standards and practices in the concert industry, it was taking a toll on all of us. Bob asked once, "What would have happened if The Who's roadies quit?" Paul said that as long as he kept the roller coaster rolling fast enough, no one could jump off. But it had slowed down, and slowed just enough that three of the seven, and then Mars, making it four, had leapt. I read somewhere that Paul reckoned that I got in when it was fun and got out when it ceased to be fun. Sounds to me like it was only fun when I was there. And honestly, I kind of wanted to be T.M.

Sometimes I regret not going on that last tour and seeing Paul and Tommy walk offstage into the Chicago sunset. Once more picking up their broken gear or finishing the final song in front of a perplexed audience. But in Omaha, a ten-year-old kid was learning the chords to "Here Comes a Regular" from his older brother while down in Muscle Shoals, the son of a famous bass player had realized he didn't have to wait until the midnight hour or live up to his father's string of hits to follow his own dream, and in Owensboro, Kentucky, a gonzo cowpunk who had seen the 'Mats' onstage carnage in Cincinnati was high as hell and buying a Marshall.

Somehow, my now-checkered reputation would allow me to help facilitate the dreams of hundreds of new bands in a crumbling gin joint that would feel like an indie-rock Ellis Island in the Midwest. One by one, I would open a beer for someone who would tell me a different version of the same story—that it was a Replacements show (whether it was great or crap) that had been the inspiration to start a band. For good or bad, the Replacements had fulfilled their promise to me and kicked the door down. That kid in Omaha would start his own label, put out music for his own reasons, and one day come to me for guidance as he stepped into arenas himself. Those southern boys would go on to release rock operas.

Oddly enough, everyone I knew who had told me it was insane to get in the van in the first place now couldn't believe I was getting out. But I could see the writing on the door, and I'd hit the glass windshield on this gig. The band was beholden to advance payments by publishers, merchandisers, and labels that would cast them aside the next day in order to kiss up to the next kid in town. Music journalist Jack Rabid once said it best to me at a Soul Asylum show on the Lower East Side. He pointed out to me that in dive bars and house parties I would meet the coolest people in each town—the record clerks who hung flyers for the promoter and volunteer stagehands and kids camped out in the lot—everyone was there for the same reason.

With the Replacements it had become union stooges and sleazy bag-men fronting for corporate bosses, selling overpriced tickets to ostenta-tious frat boys and obsessive fanboys who wanted me only as a conduit to their wanting to be a part of the scene. In those last tours, sitting in cinder-block rooms in the back of hockey arenas was no more comfortable than the filthy dressing rooms in the overused and underscrubbed clubs I loved so much. Like Paul said, "The ones who love us least are the ones we die to please."

If it's any consolation, I don't understand either.

ACKNOWLEDGMENTS

Although this book was written out of desperation and not dedication, it is nonetheless a heartfelt memory of my time spent with great artists and friends. If by chance you were there during one of these events and feel that your version of the truth is slightly or totally different from my reminiscence, I would not be surprised. We view our lives through our own eyes, filming a mental motion picture in which we appear as the narrator or perhaps even the star. I ask you to look past my extravagance and yarn spinning, and recognize my right to self-express and perhaps self-absorb.

To all the innkeepers and bar stool buddies who endured my long-winded workings of these stories and still paid for my drinks, drove me home, or lent me your couch, you have a special place in my heart.

To all the fellow travelers who got in the van or hopped on the bus, I want to convey my deepest gratitudes and sympathies, along with heart-felt apologies. If you feel left out or slighted in any way, chill out man, you'll get over it.

To the myriad of biographers, professional writers, and eyewitnesses who may have felt that I was arrogant or remiss by not participating in their projects and sing-a-longs, I can only say you should have been there, it was awesome.

One more thing. If I may be so bold as to quote Marco Polo, one of, if not the, greatest travelers and seekers of all time, who on his death bed was reported to have said: "I did not write half of what I saw, for I knew I would not be believed."

Bill Sullivan has been a roadie, guitar tech, and tour manager since the 1980s. Since his time with the Replacements, he has worked with countless artists, including Soul Asylum, the Jayhawks, Run Westy Run, Bright Eyes, M. Ward, Jim James, Yo La Tengo, Cat Power, Spoon, the New Pornographers, Neko Case, Syl Johnson, and Jimmy Vaughan. As a talent buyer for the 400 Bar on the West Bank, he brought bands like the White Stripes, Drive-By Truckers, and Elliott Smith to Minneapolis.